DEAR WILL + RAMONA,
HERE IT IS! HOT OFF THE PRESS! THIS IS THE
CULMINATION OF THE IDEA THAT STARTED MOVING
ON WILL'S 50TH B-DAY (10-31-93, IN CASE YOU FORGOT).
IT'S SUCH A WONDERFUL FEELING TO HAVE FRIENDS
LIKE YOU. THANKS FOR YOUR FRIENDSHIP + SUPPORT.
ENJOY !
LOVE,
Mark

Wholistic

Taxes

Good advice you never thought you would hear from a CPA.

Mark G. Maughan, CPA, MBA
& Daniel Wilson

Library of Congress Catalog Card Number: 96-94805
ISBN 1-57502-319-9

To order additional copies
please call 714/962-1600.

For information about a writer
to assist with your book, call:
Greenberg Business Services, Inc. 714/261-8450

Printed by
Morris Publishing
P. O. Box 2110
Kearny, NE 68847
1-800-650-7888

DEDICATION BY DANIEL WILSON

To Yvette, with gratitude for your patience
and admiration for your courage.

DEDICATION BY MARK G. MAUGHAN

This book is dedicated to Liza—the one I love.

Table of Contents

Introduction

Economics is so concerned with counting and itemizing that it has lost sight of the one component, almost unmeasurable, that makes all economic activity possible: human relationships.

—**Hampden-Turner & Trompenaars** in *The Seven Cultures of Capitalism*

Wholistic taxes is a term I invented to describe an approach to income taxes that addresses the whole person. All financial decisions involve emotions, budgetary needs and restraints, and tax implications. Sound decisions must be based on a consideration of all three components, and too often financial advisors ignore the emotional impact of their advice.

This book is dedicated to restoring unity among this trinity of emotions, practicality, and income taxes as they influence your budget. I hope reading this book will produce more peace of mind and more prosperity in your personal life. I also hope it will increase your confidence about serving as a role model in your business and political circles.

We have severe national problems in this country. Our government will not solve these problems until we, as citizens, make our priorities clear to those who govern, and show them that we support them when they make tough decisions in our best interests.

The finances of our nation are tangled in a web of conflict and confusion. The reasons for this are many, and this book addresses just two of them. The first is that those who govern are attempting to please a diverse and noisy constituency with overlapping and contradictory demands. Efforts to please this constituency all too often produce soft, evasive behavior that is a parody of leadership. The only path through this confusion is to restate and reaffirm our priorities.

The second reason our nation's finances flirt with disaster is that many of our citizens, particularly the young, are not properly taught about money and how to handle it. They become poorly informed voters who put the wrong people in office. Uneducated adults cannot properly teach the young about money. This book deals with money basics in a firm, but sympathetic manner with the intention that readers will then be able to do the same.

Wholistic taxes provides an evolving view of how personal values regarding money, corporate behavior, and the condition of our nation are interrelated. The daily newspaper headlines that were published during its preparation helped shaped the book. Wholistic taxes is necessarily attuned to current events.

This book begins on a decidedly philosophical note partly in order to balance the sterility that most of us associate with financial advice. Money is not a purely academic subject. It touches us in profoundly emotional ways. Greed is real. Fear is real. In order to come to a deep understanding of money in our personal and public lives, we must acknowledge and deal with our passions about money in addition to tallying correctly the debits and credits on the ledger sheet.

In my experience, the people who are most successful with money recognize that there is order, but not total predictability to money. They approach money with confidence, and they never lose themselves in it. They enjoy it, but they never measure themselves by it. The people I know who are comfortable with money are a small minority. If you are one of those few, I encourage you to mentor others who are not.

Society's attitudes towards money are constantly changing. Consider our view of banks. Our parents knew banks as palatial buildings, ornate with marble floors and towering columns. This image of banks is fading as banking becomes more of an electronic function, and more abstract. Banks as monuments demand that we speak in hushed and reverent tones. In these buildings, which dwarf most churches, it is clear what is important. The ponderousness of these places and the stark, chilling atmosphere heavy with some unnamed intimidation, create the illusion that human beings control money. They also sanitize and conceal to some degree the rawness of the power that falls to the possessor of vast sums of money.

It is frightening to lack for money, especially when we are unable to buy essentials. Our notion of what is essential is highly elastic and is itself a subject of much controversy such that we are on guard most of the time. We wonder how other people cope. The success of television soap operas may stem from our desire to see that the rich suffer too, and perhaps even more than the rest of us. Is their pain traceable to their money? Soap operas indulge our fantasy that money is dangerous and ominous.

To deal with this bundle of mystery, to tame it enough that we can conduct our ordinary affairs of life within the haunting reach of its shadow, we assume a posture. There are countless postures ranging from the authoritative, pin-striped, iron-jawed investment expert who speaks a strange language, to the giddy bride who mocks her own lack of self-confidence by wearing a t-shirt that proclaims "I can't be out of money, I still have checks left!" Popular women's magazines are brimming with pat answers to tough questions from perky, innocent readers. It is as though Gidget and beach-blanket movies were on the same level as sound financial planning.

Wholistic Taxes takes the position that restoring a balance by knowledgeably claiming our right place in the world will restore a wholesomeness that has declined in visibility and stature in our nation. It is tempting to blame government for our problems, as many people do. I am convinced that "blaming" is obsolete.

The Japanese were the first business community to listen to people like W. Edwards Deming, a man who taught them to fix the problem, not the blame. It is time to return to a simple awareness of responsibility without simplistic judgments of right and wrong. We make things work the way they do, and government is our reflection. *Wholistic Taxes* is concerned with the ripple effect that our personal actions set in motion. *Wholistic Taxes* presents an empowering point of view that dwells on our ability to create our financial reality. By taking charge of our own affairs, we influence the neighborhood and the nation.

What is not widely known is that remedies exist for our social problems. We are not unlike the unfortunates in third-world countries who die of ugly diseases for lack of a few pennies worth of vaccine that sits unused on shelves in laboratories in the western world. We can solve our raging problems of welfare, gang violence, and bulging prisons by using knowledge that is already available. This knowledge is known to scholars and poets, to grandparents and to mystics. In our frenzy to get information, we sometimes forget to seek wisdom. Jesus said the truth shall make us free. The truth about solving our social problems, and these are expensive problems as measured both by dollars and pain, is that remedies exist. By learning about them, we put them into motion.

The problems we face today are not new. How exciting it would be to solve our old, tired problems and discover new ones! We need to renew our vision of the future. Our village elders are all too often rich inside-traders and white-collar hooligans who fail us as role models. We need to restore wisdom and compassion to a visible and honored place in our community. This happens when all of us speak our mind. We all have something to say. We must say it. This book is an effort to sound the bell for a new vision of how things can be.

In writing this book I have drawn both inspiration and text from a series of books compiled and written by Mary Ellen Stoddard Smith that trace the history of the families from which I spring. I draw particularly from the book *From Wales to Washington,* which chronicles in particular the life of my great grandfather, Joseph Howell. He had ten children and served in politics in Utah and the United States House of Representatives for seven terms. He never was confident he would be reelected and lived in rented lodgings in the capital, twelve of them over the years. I am deeply moved by the eulogy to him published by the *Herald Republican* on July 20, 1918, and I have repeated it in Appendix B of this book. Reading it will give you some insight into his character. Mary Ellen was assisted by many members of my extensive and well-documented family. I thank her and her many helpers for creating this wonderful resource. I was also greatly inspired by his insights on writing. As a first time author myself, his words mean a lot to me. I have reproduced them in Appendix B. If you have thoughts of writing your own book, you will enjoy his words.

In contrast to my book, hers begins with the phrase "No copyright. Reproduction and distribution are freely encouraged." I am grateful for her work and want to acknowledge her contribution to my ability to appreciate my heritage.

Nothing is more exciting to me than things that work, things that do what they say they will do. The wholistic approach to money assumes interconnectedness of money management for the individual, for our families, and for our government. It shows how to reconcile heart and head on money issues. It shows you how to get the most out of your money, and how be a good citizen who influences public policy without quitting your day job.

I wrote this book to empower people. I know that anything that is examined is changed by the experience. Just throwing light on a situation improves it. The budget mess we have in Congress can only maintain itself under the cover of darkness. Government, like society, is a constellation formed from the stars of our individuality. The only way to achieve meaningful change in government is to change our expectations and our actions.

Wholistic Taxes is an adventure for me that grew out of years of candid sharing and painstaking work that my clients and I have done together to improve their financial affairs. Wholistic taxes will, I am convinced, make your financial life better and more rewarding. I justify the purchase of a book if I get one useful idea from it. I have worked to make this book at least that valuable. My job in this book is to introduce you to a better way to manage your financial affairs. Each chapter is intended to be able to stand alone.

This means that you can read chapters in any order you choose. It also means that you will find some ideas presented in more than one chapter. This is inevitable since I am tracing the ripple effect of actions that occur on the individual's level and which ultimately influence national affairs. I have endeavored to make this repetitiveness informative rather than tiring.

I have what many people consider an odd combination of education in accounting and psychology. That education contributes to my ability to discern the struggles people go through in their efforts to manage their finances in such a way that they achieve peace of mind.

I write from my vantage points as a Certified Public Accountant, father, grandfather, and citizen of the USA. My education and credentials include an MBA (1976), and degrees in chemistry (1973) and psychology (1978). I became a CPA in 1983 and a partner in the firm of Brown & Maughan the same year. I obtained a certificate in Advanced Personal Financial Planning in 1985. My practice is almost entirely taxes; I specialize in tax planning.

My education is unusually diverse because I find that diversity helps me clarify otherwise unmanageable concepts. Chemistry appeals to me because of its precision and the certainty of the answers it provides. Chemistry and math produce answers that are right or wrong, like accounting. I love the periodic table of elements for its elegance. It portrays a series of elements, each with one more proton and one more electron than the previous one. The familiar world of our everyday affairs is built on these subtle differences.

I went on to study psychology because I had some GI Bill left after finishing my other work. Going to classes that were about people was a revelation that helped me tremendously. I was there to learn about motivating other people, but I learned more about myself than I had ever known before. In school, everyone is thinking about the future, about how they will use what they are learning, and about what they must learn in order to fulfill their expectations for the future. Money management is like that; it has to be focused on future plans and expectations.

In spite of a childhood that was necessarily frugal because of my dad's commitment to medical school, I only began saving money in a methodical way when I turned forty. I have saved more each year since than in all the years previous, so I know what changing one's money habits is like. Writing this book is both a labor of love and proof that my horizons continue to expand. Furthermore, I am proud to announce that in 1994, my partner Hallet F. Brown celebrated his 40th anniversary as a CPA.

Thank you for your interest in *Wholistic Taxes.*

> Mark G. Maughan
> Fountain Valley, California
> E-mail taxxbiz@aol.com
> http://www.so-cal.com/taxxbiz

Daniel Wilson

Courage involves speaking up. To my mind, the most courageous people speak up without preaching or bragging. The people who have mastered their subjects are capable of mildness. They tell the truth, they respect simplicity. Mark Maughan is like that. I was pleased and honored to be asked to put his ideas on paper.

Mark's frequent advice to me during my visits to his office as a client left me feeling eager to apply his advice, but uncertain how to get past sticking points that made some of it difficult to use. I knew that his advice was sound, but I needed a more hands-on approach to implementing it. I needed more pictures to illustrate the concepts. I needed more exercises and lists and tools for self-examination. You will find much of this material in this book. It has been helpful to me, and our goal has been to make it helpful to you as well.

> Daniel Wilson
> Huntington Beach, California
> http://www.so-cal.com/writingbiz
> E-mail words@greenberggroup.com

Note: This book is written in the first person singular for the sake of simplicity. It represents a consensus between the authors. Mark provides the financial expertise.

Wholistic Taxes is meant to be a starting point to heighten your sense of personal power. Many references to other books are intended to encourage additional reading.

We have expressed many numbers with zeros to make a point. $1 billion is a euphemism, albeit it a mild one. A trillion is 1,000 billion.

When we use first and last names it is with the permission of the person whose story we are telling, or it is an account that is public knowledge already. When we use a first name only, it is a disguise to protect the privacy of the individual.

Section I
The power of our belief system and point of view

Chapter One: Interconnectedness

Mother objected to a certain man coming to dinner. He was a political rival—having run against Father in the last campaign. Mother said, "I won't have him in the house—Why he told terrible lies about you—I heard him myself." Father just said, "That's politics, my dear—you have to expect it," and the man came to dinner.
—**Vic Howell on his father**

We invent our own reality. Whether you ask a twentieth century quantum physicist or read centuries-old volumes of poetry and religious texts, you will find agreement that the questions we ask determine what we see. Our brains select data from the wealth of information available to us based on its relevance to the questions for which we seek answers. The biblical admonition "seek and you shall find" is now supported by hard science. Science calls our assumptions *models,* and religion calls them *faith.* The result is the same. What we believe has an uncanny way of coming true. Whether you believe you can or you can't, you're usually right.

One of the most difficult things about money is that it requires us to open our eyes to the obvious. We put answers squarely in front of ourselves, right in the language we use every day, then we ignore it. For example, we refer to being out of money as being *broke*. Broke comes from the verb break, which means to violently sever a connection. Money itself is *currency*, something that flows between us and the community in a current. Break the link with the community and the supply of money ends. Prosperity is directly related to interconnectedness. All the high-sounding economic terms in the world do not disguise the simple truth that prosperity is the wholesome (unbroken) flow of energy (current) among all of us. Break the flow of current and poverty is the result. The key to prosperity is to restore the broken links, to make ourselves whole again.

Dr. Deepak Chopra invites those who read his slender book *Creating Affluence* to choose luxury as a lifestyle. I agree. I define luxury as having enough of everything that matters to you. It is the notion that luxury is only for the few that prompts us to continue to revise our definition of the word in such a way that luxury is defined as that which is out of reach, or unnecessary, or both. Like the mythological Tantalus, whose punishment was to find the ripe fruit pulled away as he reached for it, and the quenching water lowered as he bent to drink, so many people think that luxury is a cause for envy rather than an invitation to grow.

We tend to minimize the importance of what we do well because, over time, it has come to seem easy. We tend to exaggerate the difficulty of what others do well, although they learned in a way that is also open to us. It is helpful to know that money management is learned, and just as you now do things well, you can also learn to manage money well. Your style won't be identical to that of others, but it will work for you.

This book is intent upon guiding you to a practical, working knowledge of money. I urge you to be rich and to enjoy luxury, however you may define it. I am convinced that the United States is extremely rich. We disguise that condition by diverting people to jail, welfare, an inflated government work force, and many other nonproductive activities. We also buy too many military weapons. In spite of this enormous waste, we are sufficiently rich as a country to put color televisions in 96 percent of our homes, and to fill our highways to overflowing with automobiles.

We seem to be lost in busy activity. We have lost much of our sense of connection. Our connection through time is near zero. Few of us can name our great grandparents or what they did to earn a living. Few of us keep a journal of our days and weeks, our passing moods and concerns. The brevity of our lives is exaggerated by our learned indifference to the past. When the past disappears, so does the future. We fail to plan. The future seems unreal and therefore not worth the time and effort required to create a plan for it.

A visitor from Mars might be baffled by our belief system in the United States. It would seem that we believe that society must have a few rich people and lots of poor people, that this is the natural order and can be no other way. It would see that we believe it rehabilitates people to send them to jail where it takes the tax revenues of four responsible citizens to support each irresponsible citizen. The Martian would wonder why our faith in this concept is so strong that jail populations are many multiples of those in other modern countries, and growing faster than we can erect (and fund the operation of) new prisons. Prison time is our treatment of choice for an enormous range of violations from self-inflicted wounds like drug use, to white-collar crimes that are often the moral equivalent of spelling errors. Prison ranks reached 1,000,000 in 1994, plus nearly half again that many held temporarily in jails for various reasons.

Kathleen Brown, a 1994 candidate for the California governor's seat, proposed sterner measures for graffiti vandals. She suggested making graffiti a felony based on the premise that graffiti is a "death warrant" issued by one gang to another. She also suggested that convicted graffiti vandals lose their license to drive for a year. This might not prevent them from driving, but it would make them ineligible for car insurance, should any of them have an inclination to buy it, and would therefore guarantee an increase in the risk to all drivers of being hit by an uninsured motorist.

A fondness for the quick fix

Being seriously in debt is as American as apple pie, automobiles, and MTV, yet it happened quickly, seemingly out of nowhere. Credit card debt started four years after the baby boom generation itself. The credit card was invented in 1950 by Alfred S. Bloomingdale. Its first appearance came as the Diner's Club Card, and it started a revolution. The generation that would later love brie and go-go dancing liked credit. This fondness for spending money they had not yet earned provided a base of acceptance for the government to do the same. The baby boom generation, those 76,000,000 souls born from 1946 to 1964, accepted a premise about money that changed the way government operated. The future "yuppie" generation started having too much fun to be serious about politics, which are often dull and boring. We have no firsthand memory of the Great Depression, an event that left an indelible mark on those who lived through it. The prospect of tomorrow seems remote to many of us.

We have grown vague about the role of responsibility in the world, and seemingly obsessed with protecting our rights. We seem to be overburdened with responsibility ourselves, yet we hear constantly about the crowd that gets a free ride at our expense. Fathers across the country leave their homes and refuse to pay child support. Money is tied closely to responsibility in the grand scheme of things, and confusion about one inevitably affects the other. Politicians are notorious for handing out cash to win friends for themselves. We call such handouts pork barrel projects. They give our money to their friends.

Our fondness for product liability suits demonstrates that we want to take risks, but we want someone else to pay if the risk materializes into a loss. As a nation, we are squeamish. We shy away from the responsibility that goes with saying no. We don't have a plan for the future, but maybe the lottery will make us rich and eliminate the need for a plan. We like television personalities like Rush Limbaugh to rant and rave on our behalf. It makes us feel as though we have expressed ourselves, and creates a smoke screen that hides our disconnectedness from the processes of government and citizenship.

The heroic, individualistic culture of the United States is slowly warming to the idea that each of us operates within a system. In a survey of key executives, 99 percent of American executives expected to switch jobs before retirement. Only 41 percent of Japanese felt that way.[1] Our detachment goes further than our employer. We think it is proper to run a company that knowingly pollutes the same river our children swim in after school, or to generate nuclear wastes that nobody wants stored in their neighborhood for the next millennium. We believe that earning money is a greater badge of honor than respecting the earth. We think that we can boycott the voting booth election after election without weakening our system of government. We think we can demand change from our politicians without supporting those who must implement the change by accepting their decisions to end our special allowances and favors. We pretend that we function independently. We adamantly deny that we are part of a system. We resist the responsibility which that knowledge brings.

W. Edwards Deming, the man credited with teaching quality to the Japanese, made a strong case for the dangers of tinkering with a system, any system. Americans like to tinker, to medicate the symptom instead of the disease. He called for what he termed "deep wisdom" about any system for which we may have responsibility. Deming's approach to quality is directly relevant to the issues of government and taxation that we face today, and I encourage readers to make themselves familiar with Deming's concepts. I particularly recommend *Dr. Deming, The American Who Taught The Japanese About Quality*, written by Rafael Aguayo.

My point is that most of what we demand that politicians do is *tinkering* in Deming's sense of the word. Pass this bill, fund this program, outlaw that practice. Politicians are prevented from making fundamental changes by a *systemic resistance* that originates with us. Politicians cannot change this country until we change ourselves as individuals. All demands that we place on politicians to produce change is mere posturing on our part until we support change on an intimate level in our own individual and family lives. It is possible to change this country only when we practice what we preach.

David Calleo, in his book, *The Bankrupting of America*, refers to tinkering this way:

> Small wonder that every administration since the 1960s, trying to ride out the swirling events of its time, has shrunk from cures that seemed worse than the disease and convinced itself that time and a little adjustment would eventually repair the country's problems.

The operative phrase "convinced itself" is a root of lying and avoiding. We are losing our grip on candor, to say the least. America is an increasingly dishonest place, and the dishonesty is increasingly public. A sports agent, a baseball scout, writing anonymously for *Worth* magazine, said, "I am an agent in an industry that is in my judgment among the most corrupt in the United States today."

One third of government employees are hired to check on and audit their peers and you. Bureaucracies assume people are unreliable. Is private enterprise better? Prudential Bache was sued by thousands of small investors for, among other things, lying to them about limited partnership investments. The company is spending more than $200,000,000 to repay customers who were cheated. The fiasco resulted in the breakup of Prudential from Bache, the former becoming Prudential Investments. Prudential is the second-largest holder of real estate in the nation.

Many of our young people look to Hollywood for role models. The movie industry has an honesty problem according to some sources. The *Los Angeles Times* reported on the relationship between Hollywood and the press:[2]

> "The environment is as toxic as it can get," said Columbia Pictures publicity chief Mark Gill. "Every time a new reporter comes to the Hollywood beat, they get immediately overwhelmed by the cacophony of lies. One of the consequences of the lack of truth-telling is the enormous level of hostility between Hollywood

and the press. There's so much distrust now that it's dehumanizing. It makes it easy for many reporters to write something extraordinarily nasty about someone, to a large degree because they don't think of them as real people anymore."

Mistrust hits closer to home than Hollywood. John Gatto, New York City's Teacher of the Year for 1989, wrote: "The truth is that schools don't really teach anything except how to obey orders."[3] He blames what he calls the dehumanization of the school environment for producing negative attitudes in children and asks, "Is it any wonder that the children I teach are indifferent to the adult world, have almost no curiosity, and have a poor sense of the future, of how tomorrow is inextricably linked to today?"

Are schools dehumanizing? In the busy, largely upscale Southern California town of Huntington Beach, police dogs are brought onto Huntington Beach Union High School campus to sniff for drugs. A UCLA Law School associate dean points out, "...minors have [fewer] constitutional rights than full citizens and their rights are further constrained in the setting of the school system."[4] Wait until those kids get into political office. If we, who were raised in the era of Ozzie and Harriet and had free access to airports and airplanes, are bringing dope-sniffing dogs to school, what will our kids take for granted? What will they build on the foundation we have created for them?

One of my clients criticized the school system to a friend of his who is vice principal of a high school. He criticized the prevailing priorities within the educational system. He said they were backwards. He said that high schools were built on the same blueprint as prisons, using bells to move captive people from place to place, and making them serve time rather than measuring their progress. The vice principal invited him to spend a day with her on campus to get a closer look at modern reality. She was sure he would see things differently afterward. The invitation was essentially to put up or shut up. He commented to me after his day in school: "This bright, expensively educated woman spent at least half that day patrolling the playground, directing bus traffic in the school parking lot, dispensing punishment, and reviewing rules and guidelines for restraining students. Clearly the emphasis was on controlling students, not educating them."

At least eight high schools in Long Beach, California have sealed student lockers permanently and several nearby schools are following suit. Principals want to eliminate this obvious hiding place for drugs and guns.[5] In response to complaints that books are too heavy to lug around, some campuses issue students two copies of each book, one for class and one for home use. Is that a good investment? Is the whole program the example we want to set for teenagers in conflict resolution? If the need for security has spread from airports to high school lockers, what is next? How far will we retreat from genuine problem solving?

Nationally, about 75 percent of Americans graduate from high school. West Virginia has the worst record at 69 percent. Utah has the best at 90 percent. California has the largest classes in America with 28 students per teacher and has a citizenry that is 80 percent high school educated. Making high schools more prison-like does not bode well for increasing these numbers.

In the quaint coastal town of Avila Beach, California, Unocal operates a series of oil storage tanks. These tanks developed leaks which the company learned of in 1977. By 1994 the situation was so advanced that the only remedy was major excavation of the center of town in order to clean up the damage.[6] Exxon has an ugly history of spills and destruction. What does it do to the value systems of people who work for these companies? What does it say about our values and leadership that a company defiles the neighborhoods in which it operates and remains silent about it? Is it any surprise that government is selfish and unresponsive if our major corporations openly show contempt in this way?

The IRS does not trust taxpayers, probably with good reason. The IRS estimates that "about 17 percent of the tax dollars due each year are not being collected" according to commissioner Margaret Richardson, speaking to a professional organization of CPAs in 1994. They depend greatly on their powers of coercion to get paid. Mistrust is built into many of our institutions.

Our politicians are a creation of an environment of lies and mistrust. How could it be otherwise? If dishonesty is taken for granted in the business world as the daily newspapers say it is, how can we expect those who govern us to take a stand for honesty? We prepare new generations for a dishonest way of life when we build controls into our schools that assume the students cannot be trusted. We must reaffirm our expectations of truthfulness.

Premise #1 of Wholistic Taxes
All personal choices are significant to society.

Scientist Danah Zohar suggests that the widespread feeling of personal impotence in the face of enormous national and global problems springs from the erosion of respect we have for ourselves as humans. She writes:[7]

> ...we have lost our sense of where the deep roots of our humanity lie, and hence we have lost touch with the source of our own efficacy as personal and moral agents. We no longer know what gives us the authority to act. We don't know from whence comes either mandate or capacity to act.

A feeling of ineffectiveness translates into permission to take shortcuts in our private lives and to abandon, or at least shelve, concerns as citizens. We can only reassert ourselves as citizens by restoring our sense of self at the local level.

The scientific community has an articulate spokesman who recognizes the value of village elders. Jonathan Mann teaches at the Harvard School of Public Health. His assignment there includes devising ways to recognize emerging epidemics and pandemics. (Epidemics become pandemics when they spread over a larger region.) One of the difficulties with stopping disease is that it isn't recognized until it reaches a certain threshold of visibility.

Mann wants to rely less on traditional test-tube approaches to detection and more on interdisciplinary methods. Instead of watching the health of sentinel animals, and running lab tests, he wants to talk to grandmothers. He says they are often the first to notice when a disease appears. He counts on them to put diseases into perspective so that new illnesses can be distinguished from the old ones.[8]

So it can be with issues of money. Laboratory tests and elaborate, computer-generated indexes have their place. Amid all this, however, the sage opinion from the seasoned veteran of many cycles is often the best early warning system of all.

Our relationship with government and politics

Can California buy its own breakfast? Any public school in California, as this is being written, can offer a subsidized breakfast program. "Education officials," wrote the *Los Angeles Times*, "have renewed a school-to-school battle to get more districts to offer breakfast." They want to bring 300 more schools into the program. The program is funded "with mostly federal funds." Can California citizens buy bagels for their own kids? The desire to feed children is admirable, but is it wise to involve the federal government in the task? The government has not demonstrated that it is skilled nor efficient in handling local issues. Giving Washington authority over eggs and toast for kids is like trying to teach a gorilla to do needle point.

Politics and religion are often explosive topics for conversation. I believe there are two underlying reasons for this. The first is that we have largely forgotten how to resolve conflicts. The second is that organizations whose job it is to handle many of our tough issues have defaulted their responsibilities. Their default leaves a vacuum. Citizens now look to the government to perform tasks that are properly the domain of family and neighborhood organizations. How else could child care become an issue of federal concern to the extent that Clinton's crime bill had millions of dollars for things the Boys' Club or YWCA or high school sports or drama clubs were designed to do? Why do battered spouses need a helping hand from Washington? It is apparently because their is none on their block.

Our social institutions are complex because they are constellations in which we are the individual stars. Social institutions concentrate the abilities and talents of their members. Their potential exceeds our powers of imagination, yet all too often they seem numb and brutish. When our social institutions fail to tap into the power of their members, individuals may become passive or resort to anger when facing a challenge.

Citizens are quick to look for a father figure to make things right in the world. The government is often pressed into this role, one for which it is poorly suited. The government spends tax money trying to do something, anything, to please a distant, diverse, nervous, and often angry constituency. The federal government will never be successful at resolving home-and-hearth issues. Politics will be a messy and painful subject for both politicians and for citizens until politics trims its agenda back to appropriate political issues.

Matters of simple courtesy are deemed "politically correct." George Orwell wrote a book called 1984, one of the classic books about government getting unpleasantly involved in personal affairs. The current phrase "politically correct" is distinctly Orwellian. The government must return to governing if this country is to work well. This will only happen when families, neighborhoods, and cities reclaim their responsibilities.

The life of the community is propelled by the actions and expectations of the individual. This means that all action, including that which is commonly mistaken as inaction, affects the common good. Apathy is the *act* of doing nothing. On the other hand, all individual actions make a difference.

We take action at the level of the mundane. I recall my first work experience at the Dominguez Hills campus of Cal State University back in 1972. It was considered prestigious to have a corner office, as it still is. We had the four corners of the executive floor occupied by the president, vice president of academic affairs, vice president of administration, and the business manager. It took more than a minute to walk the full length of the hall, and communication was poor among these key executives. President Donald Gerth came up with a clever solution. He redefined prestige. He said that true prestige is having an office close to the president.

Two executives moved next door to his office. Under this new arrangement all offices were within a one minute walk, and the three with the most frequent interactions were adjacent.

This move benefited the whole university by making the executive team more productive. It made the daily lives of the executives easier, and it avoided wounds to egos by a clever face-saving device.

Consider the example of Laker tickets at the Los Angeles Forum. The seats courtside, where Jack Nicholson and Arsenio Hall sit, cost $500 each, and there are none available. No matter how many empty seats there are in the balcony, these seats are full. When Jerry Buss bought the team, he installed an owner's box. He had it built at the end of the arena. He sits in the front of it, and there are seats behind him where guests can sit and later boast of having sat in the owner's box. Any complainers who would rather sit on the floor with the movie stars can expect to be asked, "If these seats are good enough for the owner of the team, aren't they good enough for you?"

We constantly redefine prestige. Every generation seeks to modify the definition. In the 1980s the "yuppies" were fond of conspicuous consumption of an imitative sort. The pendulum will eventually swing back to more personal, idiosyncratic, and imaginative definitions of prestige. We can hasten that. It begins with simple efforts to become more connected.

These efforts take place at home, in the office, and where we play games. We fail to encourage imagination among our children. The market brims with toys that are so laden with color, features, and detail that the child has little opportunity to add to them. Too much of the task of the imagination was done at the factory. Naturally the child tires of the toy quickly because someone else already had the fun the toy was meant to provide. The long term price is higher still. The child fails to develop powers of imagination. It is imagination that provides the means of creating new solutions to old problems so that we need not imitate the past.

Every decision makes a difference, and our expectation of the outcome is the most influential force we can bring to bear on our affairs. Rejuvenating this nation is about raising our expectations, yours and mine. It is also about insisting that others who are accountable to us do the same.

As we discover more about the power of our belief system to shape our experience of reality, we are quicker to examine those beliefs. It is especially important to examine our beliefs about money and taxes. I argue throughout this book that government is our reflection, not our ruler. As we change, government changes. We can only fix our national problems by starting the change in our own back yard, watching it ripple through the companies we run and which employ us, and outward to the halls of Congress.

> **Premise #2 of Wholistic Taxes:**
> **Prosperity is a measure of how our relationships are working.**

Chapter Two: Priorities

A dinner invitation to the White House should be acknowledged immediately, accepted if possible, and all other invitations canceled in its favor.
— **Congressional Club Year Book of 1913**

I play racquetball all year, including the height of tax season when I work from 10 a.m. until past midnight seven days a week. I have always felt that protecting my recreation time was appropriate, but it took an example from the club itself to help me put it into words. The club opened with 25 courts; it was 100 percent devoted to racquetball. Eventually it converted one court to an aerobics room. The logic was that the first aerobics room was a higher priority than the twenty-fifth racquetball court. Then it converted another court to a weight room. The logic was that the first weight room was more important than the twenty-fourth racquetball court.

Presently the club has 16 courts. It has changed as the interests of members changed. Racquetball is no longer played by people who simply want to appear contemporary and sophisticated, so the club needs just enough courts for players who love the game.

I consider my first racquetball session in a week to be more important than my twenty-fifth client appointment. My first meeting with my children is more important than my twenty-fourth appointment, and so on until I have trimmed back my schedule to a level that is consistent with the overall priorities in my life. I am more comfortable now that I have a way to express this method of setting priorities. Thanks to the club for providing an example. Seeing how other people cope with the same problems that face us is both informative and reassuring. The example does not have to be grand or important. It can be as simple as something done at the club where we go to play.

Our priorities, including those that affect how we spend money, are seated deeply within us. Some people save money effortlessly, and impulsive spending is all but unthinkable. Others leave money in a savings account as briefly as if it were a checking account. They find themselves always under pressure to buy things, and always out of cash with which to buy them. The same rules operate very differently among different people.

We can wrestle with behaviors all we want, but if we don't understand our underlying beliefs, symptoms reappear as soon as our attention strays to a new subject. The way we act produces the results whose collective effect we call *reality*.

Blaming ourselves for the way our lives are going adds to our anger and annoyance without making anything better. We find ourselves in the odd situation of being split into parts which argue with each other. One part wants better results, another part seems stuck in old ways of doing things. This conflict surfaces when we make New Year's resolutions—then break them. The act of threatening ourselves merely accelerates whatever action was already in place and increases the polarization between the various voices within us.

Sometimes we conceal our real reasons for the things we do. Perhaps we fear that we are not as worthy as other people. They are luckier, or smarter, or more deserving of generosity. We often mask the relationship between our behavior and our beliefs. We often make up things to explain our actions in a way that will make sense to our audience, or at least throw them off the scent. That process is called rationalizing. It is designed to make our idiosyncrasies seem rational, which means that other people can match what they see us do with something that is already familiar and acceptable to them.

Idiosyncrasy comes from Greek words and means "one's own unique mixture." We are all unique, and our ways of handling money must take that into account. One size does not fit all.

We can diagram the relationship of our beliefs and behaviors in this way.

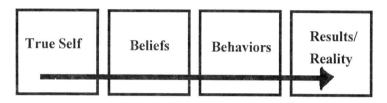

We all have beliefs about ourselves. We act in ways that express those beliefs, and our actions support our personal view of reality. That is why we can look around us and see such an amazing variety of human experience. We each act out according to what we believe to be true for us. Different actions produce different experiences of what is real.

Most of us look at our finances and think that they tell us who and what we are. Our financial situation is an experience we are having. It does not mirror our true identity. We may also think that we are our beliefs. We forget that beliefs can be amended, as they often are by caregivers and other people around us. If you know who you are, you can identify your beliefs as separate from you.

Let's take the example of a woman to whom the old line about a beer budget and champagne tastes refers. This old maxim is a playful way to describe a conflict at the level of beliefs. A person in this predicament might believe that the level of comfort she aspires to is somehow objectionable. Because it is objectionable, she will find a way to avoid achieving the level of prosperity that would provide this level of comfort. There are many ways to avoid success, but it is harder to quiet our fundamental longing to experience the life we know to be genuine for us. That which is genuine about us continues to call to us.

This woman will find her desire for champagne cropping up time after time. Since she lives on a beer budget, she will resort to roundabout methods to express her appetites. Credit can be one of those methods. The result is that her finances get out of balance, and she has now added guilt to her other problems. There is more money going out than coming in, and she mistrusts her desires. If she were a "better person" wouldn't she save more money? Still, the purchases satisfy something deep, so sorting out what it all means is confusing.

After a while she may decide that irresponsibility is characteristic of her basic nature. She adds a new belief: I am irresponsible. At this point she may discredit herself in terms of wisdom and worthiness. The solution is to identify the beliefs that are in place. This requires introspection, patience, and imagination.

I recommend that you read widely, record your thoughts daily in a journal, and ask other people about their experiences with similar concerns. Out of that will come your solution. You will find that few people know themselves or their problems well. Problems yield to imagination. When you see problems that seem impenetrable, you will also find a void of imagination.

Our thoughts shape our actions. The reverse can also be true. If you cannot identify the thoughts that are giving rise to your actions, you might try changing your actions. This is described by the cliché "Fake it until you make it." To begin to think confidently, try acting confidently. Here is a simple experiment that illustrates how this works. The next time you are in a mood that you dislike, have your body do something inconsistent with the mood. If you are depressed, make clown faces in a mirror. If you are angry, start dancing. We are unable to maintain incongruity of mood and body language for long, and the one we favor with our attention will prevail.

The difficulty of being honest

Because we live in a world in which pretense and cover-up are commonplace, we tend to fall prey to it ourselves. If you listen closely to people when they talk, you will find that they seldom tell the truth. This is not to say that they lie. Rather, they fudge, overlook, round corners, generalize, exaggerate, cushion, forget, soften, and dramatize the truth. They use figures of speech, slang, buzz words, hype and shortcuts. It is surprisingly difficult to tell the truth in a world that treats language carelessly and still expects it to serve faithfully and accurately on demand.

An hour of rigorous truthfulness a revealing experiment. You might be amazed at the obstacles to being truthful. You may be startled to really notice what people say. The gaps of logic, detail, and accuracy in what people say to you may be surprising, and their impatience with your requests for more clarity is disconcerting. "Well, YOU KNOW what I mean!" they will reply in exasperation. Finally, you are likely to discover that you cannot distinguish levels of reality within yourself.

At the deepest level we are changeless, but our beliefs are personal and subjective. Most of the effort expended by our society today is directed toward changing behaviors and results. That is why we are so tired and frustrated much of the time. We are attacking shadows on the wall, not the objects that cast the shadows. In this metaphor, it is the beliefs that cast the shadows we call reality. You can deduce your beliefs by asking, "What could I believe that would explain this behavior?" I recommend asking this question in writing, preferably in your journal.

Experts who study how people and organizations change call the process of altering surface behavior "single-loop learning." When underlying beliefs are examined and changed, the term used is "double-loop learning." Only changes that reach to the belief level are permanent.

Quality control experts teach that we cannot change results. We can only change behaviors. Like the organizational change experts, they too teach that if you don't change the underlying belief, the behavior will reassert itself endlessly. Behavior arises from our beliefs with wonderful consistency.

My client Robert did not follow a budget. He said he gave up on budgets because he was constantly breaking them, or "coloring outside the lines" as he liked to call it. He found that being reminded of his inability to change his habits was disturbing, so he quit making the effort. His spending pattern was to run out of cash before payday and resort to credit cards. Many of his expenditures were for arbitrary purchases such as meals in restaurants, books, and other items that could easily wait until payday.

Robert was frustrated with his situation. He felt trapped in this cycle because it appeared to him that reality was controlling him. Part of the reason he used credit cards was to avoid feeling trapped, yet he felt thoroughly trapped. His efforts to change failed repeatedly because he was concentrating on the visible part, not the root cause. Everything we do has a positive purpose. We just have to figure out what that purpose is.

Like many people, Robert was reluctant to examine his beliefs about what money meant to him. Gradually, though, his annoyance at his recurring problem of credit card bills was enough to drive him to investigate. He begin to ask, what belief system is supported and served by this habit of saying yes when he would be better served by saying no?

Robert discovered some deep concerns about people saying no in his life. He believed he had seen people wronged by the stinginess of people toward those who depended on them. He felt compelled to try to please people by agreeing with their plans and desires. He also was frightened by inability to participate in social activities after having been painfully shy for many years. If people wanted to go to dinner, he wanted to go to dinner with them. He had exaggerated fears of being left out. He was embarrassed by even the thought of saying he could not afford to go out. He eventually traced this bundle of fears back to an image he held of what fathering is all about. He envisioned a proper father figure as someone who always had the resources to participate, and who was quick to step to the front of any gathering, and would take charge if necessary.

He wanted to be a strong figure whose abilities and resources could stand the test of comparison to friends. To do less, he took to be a sign of weakness. He feared weakness in father figures because his own father had committed suicide, and most of the prominent males in his family had experienced financial or drug problems, or both. All of this anxiety became focused on his ability to rise to any occasion his friends and his dreams brought to him. To postpone a dinner out, or not buy the fine book that might well contain the secret to life, seemed to him like quitting, copping out, shrinking back. He could not see himself doing that. Better to face the intimidating bills than to disappoint friends. At a deep level, his belief was money was a measure of his ability to participate. Credit card purchases supported that, and he would rather face fear and inconvenience than let them down.

It took a lengthy period of counseling and introspection before Robert recognized the basic beliefs that were shaping his financial life. Things eventually did fall into place for him, I am happy to report.

How tinkering slows our progress in fulfilling priorities

The field of engineering has shed a great deal of light on the subject of achieving goals. This knowledge was developed through efforts to guide organizations to higher productivity and fewer defects. What scientists learned is that our best efforts produce a result that is approximately right. It may be 40 percent right or 99.9 percent right. Mathematicians have worked out an elaborate formula that rates quality, or accuracy, on a Sigma scale. Six Sigma is near perfect. Most companies are said to operate at three or four Sigma, which is pretty sloppy.

The degree of accuracy of any system is determined by the inherent reliability of the process in use and the number of variables that can impede the process. A ten-year-old delivery boy chucking a paper at your porch seldom provides accurate results because the motion of throwing the newspaper from a moving bicycle is inherently unreliable or inconsistent. In the first place, he is untrained in this skill. Add to that the variables of his wobbly bike, the speed and direction of the wind, and the changing weight of the paper from day to day.

Changing delivery boys, or subscribing to a different paper altogether, is not likely to produce the result of thrown papers landing squarely on your welcome mat. Change at this level is an example of what scientists call *tinkering* with the process.

A common mistake in a situation like this is to jump into tinkering in a bigger way. Yelling at the delivery boy is tried. Or we might give a bigger tip along with a request that the paper be kept out of the lilacs. We might build a larger porch. None of this works if the basic throw-from-the-street technique remains in place.

Are we willing to pay for the time it takes to get off the bike and place the periodical on the porch? Will the boy accommodate the request at any price? Will substitutes on his day off know about your special arrangement? Will they care?

Our financial goals are often set in simplistic ways like those used to solve the newspaper problem. First, we tend to be self-critical about our "lack of success." Most of us are quick to label our approximate success as a failure rather than partial success. Putting ourselves in the paper boy's shoes, we blame ourselves for not throwing more accurately. Our incentives and agreements to do better seldom hold up under pressure. This is because tinkering only scratches the surface of a problem.

What we must do to achieve our goals is to examine what we are doing without being judgmental. Instead of saying, "Stupid delivery kid!" we can look at our options. We might install a box next to the mail box to make throwing the paper irrelevant. We might purchase the paper at a news stand. We might decide to read an electronic newspaper on our computer and cancel our subscription to the hard copy. Finally, we might persuade a personal friend or relative to apply for the delivery job, someone who is accountable to us in ways that go beyond a stranger's loyalties.

Engineers have taught us to *examine* the process rather than slapping it upside the head in frustration. Identify the steps that are inherently unreliable and install new ones. To date, the illuminating advice of engineers has not reached everyone. Many of us are still getting, and accepting, advice to tinker. It is extraordinarily helpful to learn about getting to the root of problems rather than fighting with the symptoms. I know of no way to achieve goals without a basic understanding of how goal setting works. I encourage you to read any of the many wonderful books on quality control that grace bookshelves these days. They are nearly as relevant for individuals as they are for corporations.

> **Premise #3 of Wholistic Taxes:**
> **You can only change behaviors at decision points.**

The pattern of the way you handle money is the result of a series of decision points at which you chose a path of action. You might say the pattern is the result of connecting the dots. Move the dots, even one dot, and the pattern changes. Move many dots, even slightly, and the pattern changes noticeably. Move many dots a large distance and the new pattern is totally different from the old one. Most of us resist such drastic changes because we define sanity as our ability to recognize and predict our world. Drastic changes can make us feel insane. If our world is largely unfamiliar, we are momentarily stunned and disoriented. The sort of change people welcome is change that moves a few dots a small distance. That is the kind we concentrate on in this book.

I once had a problem with impulse buying. The first time I started making more than survival pay, I developed the habit of going to a discount variety store called the Treasury every payday. Once there, I would prowl the aisles to see what struck my fancy. I mostly bought cheap junk. My trip to the store was a decision point. Each time I picked something off the shelf, that was another decision point. I kept this habit until I made the decision to get married. The responsibilities of marriage made my old routines unworkable. I embarked on a new series of decisions as a result of the pressures of my new responsibility. This pressure is one of the benefits of responsibility and commitment.

My impulsiveness is still intact, but I monitor it and I have directed it to more worthy targets. I now buy books. I probably have 40 books at any given time that I have not read. I tend to explore new authors by purchasing their current book new. If I like it, I scour used book stores for their earlier work, which I buy at greatly discounted prices. I consider book purchases a virtue in contrast to the junky pieces I used to buy. The same energy that was once wasteful is now productive, at least as far as I am concerned.

Setting priorities is part of a larger program called discipline, a word which means "to prepare by instruction." We all crave a nourishing discipline. Our relationship to discipline is necessarily to submit to it, as that is its nature. Discipline is one of the classic paradoxes in life because our apparent surrender of freedom results in greater freedom. The prodigal son in the Bible rejects discipline in favor of what appears to be a higher degree of personal freedom. Instead it turns out to be a grinding, wearying path. He chose the equivalent of junk food over a balanced diet.

When he became sick of it, he longed for a more thoughtful way of life. His prodigal ways left him depleted and confused. By this time he felt unworthy and unclean as a result of the choices he had made. He wanted to return to his father, which can be taken literally and as a metaphor for discipline.

His brother resented the warm welcome he was given upon his return. The brother can be seen as a metaphor for the skeptical part of our minds that argues against changing our ways. It is the voice that says it is too late, we have gone too far already. Many people feel tainted by their financial history and want to avoid thinking about money because it stirs up guilt and remorse. These uncomfortable feelings are evidence of longing for discipline. In the metaphorical sense, the anxiety stems from a concern that bridges have been burned and that the rebellious one will not be welcomed back home. This is one of the fantasies to which people are vulnerable. It is a fantasy just as much as the notion that accumulating money enlarges a person. Recognize it as a fantasy, and it evaporates before your eyes.

Comfort zone and baseline

The role of comfort in the human experience is widely misunderstood and the subject of much disagreement. Monks, for example, avoid many comforts. They pledge to lead lives of chastity and poverty, and they commit to laborious work under stark conditions in the pursuit of spiritual growth. Many of them remain silent for extended periods of time, and they willingly subject themselves to other forms of denial that most of us would avoid.

The Beatles sang a song that said money wasn't important because you could not buy love with it. They were singing about romantic love, but the sentiment is not totally foreign to the monk's perspective. Some people say that money is the root of all evil, and that the way to contain its destructive power is to have so little of it that you can monitor all of it all the time. If no money is "idle" it is less likely to cause problems.

At the other end of the spectrum is the flamboyant rock star and the exaggerated world of high-flying Wall Street traders whose names end up in the headlines of the daily paper. Many people are convinced they would find comfort at that end of the prosperity spectrum, while others are equally convinced they can only find peace of mind somewhere between the worlds of the monk and the rock star.

Investments are something like that. You must make investments consistent with your disposition and with your long term goals in life if you aspire to be comfortable. An ambitious investor would be seriously uncomfortable having large sums of money in a passbook savings account. An investor with a modest retirement fund would be, or ought to be, filled with anxiety if this money were risked on a long-shot speculative investment.

Your baseline is your personal reference point, the values you take for granted. This baseline may be obscured by teachings superimposed on it by people and circumstances in your environment. The Great Depression surely obscured the baseline of many people, leaving them in a heightened state of anxiety that, for many of them, lasted all their lives.

A comfort zone seems like a womb to me. A womb is a

wonderful place. It is warm and safe and secure, but it has a disadvantage. It won't let you grow beyond a certain point. Many jobs are like wombs. The people in them don't quit for fear of losing their safety and security, even though they may be unhappy in their jobs.

Defining your comfort zone is a valuable exercise. It is important to identify it in order to know how to invest in a way that will bring you peace of mind. Stephen Covey's books are valuable tools for people who are defining their priorities and mapping their personal geography. *The 7 Habits of Highly Effective People* is relevant to those who are searching for peace of mind and who are struggling with money management.

In the next chapter we discuss specific exercises that help identify your baseline and which provide insight into how you set priorities.

Chapter Three: It's What You Keep That Counts

Affluence or wealth means that one is easily able to fulfill one's desires, whatever they may be...
—*Deepak Chopra, Creating Affluence*

One of the problems we face when making financial decisions is that we are often asked to follow bad advice. The first thing I review with clients is the subject of tax deductions. Deductions are not credits. Deductions save only a portion of the money you spend.

In California, when you have a fully deductible expense, you save about 35 percent in taxes. That breaks down to 28 percent federal, and 9.3 percent state taxes. You might notice that 28 and 9.3 add up to more than 35. The reason I cite 35 percent is that you will get a 2.6 percent deduction by matching up state and federal tax bills. If you spend a deductible dollar, you reduce your tax obligation by about 35 cents. I ask my clients if they would rather have a dollar or 35 cents. They think it is a trick question.

If you have a need to spend a dollar to help you in your business, then spend it. If you are spending a dollar to save 35 cents in taxes, that is poor economy. We have become preoccupied with the 35 cent tax savings at the expense of the 65 cents we would keep if we did not spend the dollar. It is better to keep 65 cents than to spend a dollar on something you don't need. Mortgage interest is an example of something you don't need. If you earn an extra $10,000 you pay another $3,500 in taxes, but you have $6,500 to add to your net worth.

The question to ask is, how hard did you have to work to gain the additional $10,000? Was it worth it to you? If you work wisely, you will reach a point where additional money is less appealing than the time you trade for it. A point comes in everyone's life when he or she needs to review the trade off between time and money. People often regret spending too little time with their families, or at the ballet, or playing ball. Less frequently do they regret not spending more time on the job.

The old slogan, "It's not what you make, it's what you keep that counts," serves to remind us that tax deductions are less important than additions to our net worth. To summarize, the goal is not to reduce taxes, the goal is to increase net worth.

Net worth goes DOWN	Net worth goes UP
You save 35% on taxes	You pay 35% in taxes
You pay 65% out of pocket	You keep 65%

The priority matrix

The priority matrix on page 38 provides a visual aid for assessing priorities. Scientists build models of how things work, and a model in helpful in tax planning, too. I encourage you to spend a few minutes with this exercise. Write in each quadrant examples of what you want to accomplish under each heading. There are no right or wrong answers, and you are only recording your views at the moment you fill it out. This is a snapshot of your outlook.

The terms are subjective, and that is part of the exercise. It is not possible to separate *experience* from *object* in an absolute sense. Owning a piece of sculpture, an object, creates an experience. The sculpture can be viewed, touched, and shared with friends. If you are the owner, the expense is in the object. If you view art in a museum, the expense, in the form of an admission price, is for the experience of observing the object. Similarly, a fine bottle of wine is tangible, but the act of drinking it is an experience. Attending a musical concert is an experience. A souvenir purchased at the concert is an object that summons memories of the experience whenever we use the object later. The ambiguity of these categories is reminiscent of the principle that light is both a wave and a particle. It all depends on how you examine it.

While these categories are not absolute, our tastes and biases can be greatly clarified by separating our priorities along these lines.

Priorities are tracked along two axes. The vertical axis connects objects and experiences. It is likely that you will feel differently about spending money on possessions and tangibles than you do about spending money for experiences and other intangibles. The definition of these terms is intriguingly fuzzy and open to interpretation. It is this very fuzziness that we must all deal with as we make financial decisions in real life. Is a fine meal an object or an experience? You have plenty of room to decide for yourself. If you have strong feelings on the subject of tangibles versus intangibles, it will affect your priorities accordingly.

After you have made enough entries that you feel your interests are clearly represented on the page, you can go back and mark pluses + by the things that you especially want, and minuses - by things that are not so important. You can carry this to any level of complexity you like, but it is not necessary to make it terribly detailed. It is helpful to assign a percentage to each quadrant to indicate its relative dominance in your life. Make certain the total of all four equals 100 percent. This is a beginning point for a map that will evolve over time. I encourage you to fill this in quickly with more emphasis on spontaneity than on "getting it right."

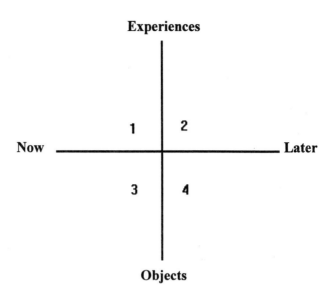

Interpreting the results

The method I recommend for interpreting the results is to simply compare them with the results recorded by other people you know. Then sit down to a leisurely, wandering conversation about your discoveries. What you are likely to find is that people differ in their notions of what "later" means. They also categorize experiences and objects in ways that are likely to differ from the way you do it. What you consider to be an object, they may consider to be an experience, and vice versa. Some people make the same entry under both headings.

Your responses will point you in the direction of discovering your values. This is the level where your efforts to change can be productive in contrast to quick fixes that encourage you to arm-wrestle with habits. I encourage you to explore this material gently rather than looking for right or wrong answers. This is an effort to draw a map of how you see your life unfolding. The very act of examining this information will help you clarify your goals and more perfectly align your priorities. I recommend that you not judge yourself. Only judge the effectiveness of behaviors. All points of view are valid, but some are more fun than others.

My client Sam owns four pieces of property, all with active mortgages. He is extremely conscientious about making his payments. He stocks his cupboard with staples: flour, rice, peanut butter and other shelf-stable edibles, so that he has food to eat during the occasional periods when he is out of cash due to the demands of his properties. He explained to me that the adjustment in lifestyle is a good idea because, thanks to his frugality now, in later life he will not have to live on flour, rice, and peanut butter.

If our plan for life marks the path to our future, the clarity and reach of our plan matters. The priority matrix addresses the questions of what people mean by the terms *now* and *later* and what they consider experiences as compared to objects. I have tested the priority matrix only in an unscientific way by asking friends and clients to fill it out. While these results are not scientifically valid, they are revealing on an anecdotal level. The priority matrix is a useful exercise that provides a point of departure for a comparison of values between partners, and I recommend it for that purpose.

Case studies

Deb's matrix

Deb blurs the line between now and later, and she assigns each quadrant an even 25 percent priority. She assigns equal importance to now and later, objects and experiences. On closer examination, her priorities for long term experiences are virtually identical to her short term priorities, and they are all short-lived, immediate gratification experiences. Her most far reaching goal in terms of experiences is a vacation. Basically, her future is indistinguishable from the present.

On the level of objects, she is preoccupied with golf. She wants balls now and clubs later. Home furnishings are desired now and later.

Dave's matrix

Dave carefully weighs his priorities. Later counts for 70 percent of his priorities, and experiences for 60 percent. Later extends as far as his grandchildren's education and how he is remembered by his family. Dave places exercise and proper eating in the category of objects, and he similarly assigns a religious goal to the category of objects.

Dave's goal in life is to feel good about his life on the day he dies. He wants God to smile on him. Dave buys his clothes used and supports nine children. Dave is heavily vested in long term rewards and in experiences. Dave's concern about rewards in the afterlife are common among churchgoing people. Anyone who postpones pleasure, and then seeks that pleasure in the form of intangibles such as divine approval is solidly in quadrant two indicating a desire for experiences later in life.

Objects now:	*10%*
Experiences now:	*20%*
Objects later:	*30%*
Experiences later:	*40%*

Robert's matrix

Robert assigns 60 percent of his priorities to experiences. The future holds different experiences than the present. He sees himself making a transition from impulse purchases now to durable goods and fine art later, but he is vague on how the transition will occur. Robert is a weak planner and becomes agitated at tax time.

Objects now:	*20%*
Objects later:	*20%*
Experiences now:	*30%*
Experiences later:	*30%*

How Robert thought of "later"

Robert's family included no role models of how to age gracefully. His father committed suicide at 46 after a mixed-up life of divorces and bankruptcies. His uncles, aunts and cousins demonstrated little interest in long term plans, and with every passing year most of them suffered more from physical deterioration and poverty. Robert, a man with a strong sense of curiosity and an analytical mind, had a difficult time conceptualizing the future, and this made saving money seem pointless.

Robert has no children, and one of the experiences he finds satisfying is picking up the dinner tab for friends. He says it makes him feel paternal. His spending habits are linked to strong emotions that run well beyond the reach of logic. His priorities, therefore, cannot be realigned with the simple administration of a bit of logic and lecture.

It was not until his forties that Robert says he developed a concept of future time. Until then his idea of "later" was the end of the month when the credit card bills arrived.

We all need to develop an awareness of our notions of time in order to understand our handling of money. People do not prepare for a tomorrow that they do not believe exists for them.

Susan's matrix

Susan has a relatively highly-skewed matrix and blurs the line between experience and personal traits. She calls confidence an experience, for example. Her long term goals extend to a wedding, family and career. She puts career and success at painting in the object category.

Objects now:	*35%*
Experiences now	*50%*
Objects later:	*5%*
Experiences later:	*10%*

Susan puts buying a house in the experience category: "buying a house and living in it" is her goal. For Susan the distinction between objects and experiences is vague at best.

Another fellow, Larry, has a passion for sport and music events. He buys Laker season tickets, attends concerts at the Hollywood Bowl several times a year, and always celebrates the occasion with a gourmet bottle of wine. Larry also rents a tiny apartment, drives a cheap car, and buys his clothes at Sears. He is firmly established in quadrant one. He wants experiences, and he wants them now.

What do you need? What is possible?

In order to set priorities you must have some idea how much of anything is enough for you and how soon you must have it. You need a map of how far into the future your plans extend. You need to grasp the relationship between what you want soon and what you want later. This provides a basis for knowing what to do first. When you have provided for a need or a want in one area of your life, you can turn your attention to lesser priorities.

We all have hundreds of decision points every day, but we are so familiar with many of them that we hardly notice them anymore. You can only change your behavior at decision points, and you can only do that if you are clear about your priorities. If you have some knowledge of Zen, you know that it involves paying attention to the choices we make.

Zen practitioners use a process called "sitting" during which the students watches his or her thoughts and notices which of them provoke a reaction. Such exercises acquaint us with our mental and emotional inventory. Pioneer psychoanalyst Carl Jung said that most people find this digging to be too much work, and so they avoid it. Scott Peck says in *The Road Less Traveled* that neurosis is the result of efforts to <u>avoid</u> the legitimate suffering that accompanies growth and learning.

As we study our values we find that we resonate to some while others seem artificial. Genuine values cannot be explained. They are elemental; they have no origins, and no component parts. They are, as children say, "just because." Why do I like sunny weather? Just because I do. Why do I like to enjoy people? Just because I do. My need for sunny weather and for companionship are genuine.

Counterfeit values can be explained. A client once told me, "I felt unworthy of success for a time because my early role models told me that doing better than they did would be an act of vanity. They often criticized my successes. Once I had an interview for an exciting job in San Francisco. When I told my mother, she just commented that she hoped my plane wouldn't crash. She resented my success. I had a thoroughly confused idea of what being boastful really was. A lot of healthy desires were mis-labeled in my family." The belief that he ought to not exceed his family's attainments was counterfeit. Once he saw that he began to make quicker progress.

Only by identifying and testing our beliefs can we distinguish the real from the unreal. At that point we are in a position to know which needs are genuine. Genuine needs have a reassuring depth and power. When we contemplate them we feel "at home."

How far is up?

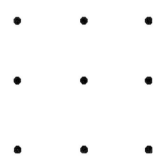

You may have seen this puzzle before. It has been a feature of psychology classes for many years. The objective is to connect all the dots with four straight lines without lifting your pencil from the paper. The solution is in the glossary under "dots." See if you can solve it. It will prepare you mentally for reading this section.

We have limits that we take for granted. We have minimums, amounts we expect will always be provided to us. There are also maximums, levels we would be startled to exceed. Most of my clients could not imagine being homeless. They assume that something would always come along to prevent that from happening. They would always respond to their circumstances in a way that would prevent that miserable experience. On the other hand, most of them have reasons to explain why they will not have wealth beyond a limit that is unique to each of them. I recommend learning as much as you can about the limits that you take for granted.

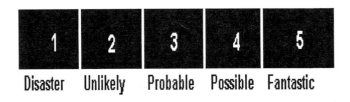

I am suggesting five zones as pictured above. Zone 5 is the Fantastic zone. The zone is characterized by winning the lottery. There are many equivalents to winning the lottery. The movie Forrest Gump dealt with some of them. He got rich in spite of himself. Turn to the analysis section that follows on the next page and list three ways you could enter this zone, three things you would start doing if you were there, and three things you would abandon. Then do the same for all the zones listed there.

Zone 4 is the zone of the Possible. You can see yourself being this rich through, perhaps, native ability and luck. Or luck and a bit of sleight-of-hand, or any other combination that suits you. It probably won't happen without some kind of special circumstance, and we all imagine the special circumstances that suit us best. Make the same list for this zone.

Zone 3 is the familiar range of the Probable. This is the zone our friends and family acknowledge. This may or may not be a particularly exciting zone, but it is predictable and secure. Make the list of things you do in this zone that are characteristic of this zone. This is difficult because you are so close to it you tend to take your activities for granted. They seem so essential, so inevitable.

Zone 2 is the zone of the Unlikely. This is the zone that inspires us to buy insurance. You are unlikely to get sick or to see your house burn down, but it might happen. Insurance, we hope, will suspend us above zone two and keep us safely and securely in zone three. Without insurance, who knows? Zone two is a hardship zone, the evil twin of the Possibility zone. We don't associate goals with this zone. It is a place to avoid.

Oddly, zone 2 is a rich and enlightening place for many people. In folklore this is the place of darkness where people learn about their most elemental values and instincts. We see rock and roll stars and movie stars enter this zone quite often. Elton John went there and comments now that he wonders how he survived the drugs and the general abuse to his body. Granted, he had money while he was there, but in all other regards, he was thoroughly mired in the zone of the unlikely.

Zone 1 is the zone of the Impossible, the nightmare, the freak show. This is the zone where homeless people, and those forgotten in third-rate nursing homes, and hard scrabble shut-ins live.

You can add a great deal of detail to your mental and emotional road maps by filling out this simple questionnaire. I encourage you to think in broad terms. Think of the attitude behind the specific action. For example, one of my entries in the possible realm is that I would buy a luxury car, and I would buy it new. The larger idea behind this is that I would begin doing things that become available to me by virtue of having satisfied a lot of the down-to-earth tasks of my life. Since first drafting this section, I have purchased a new car.

When you fill out the form, feel free to write in "buy a Lexus," but think about what that means in the larger context. I also suggest that you notice synonyms for the same thing. For example, win the lottery, get an inheritance, marry wealthy, may all mean the same thing to you: money comes from other peoples' achievement and luck. Use this exercise to examine your assumptions.

Fantastic:
Three ways I could get there:

1._____
2._____
3._____

Three things I would begin to do:

1._____
2._____
3._____

Three things I would cease to do:

1._____
2._____
3._____

Possible:
Three ways I could get there:

1._____
2._____
3._____

Three things I would begin to do:

1._____
2._____
3._____

Three things I would cease to do:

1._____
2._____
3._____

Probable
Three things that maintain this level of experience:

1._____
2._____
3._____

Three things I do that are typical of this level:

1._____
2._____
3._____

Three things I could do that are atypical of this level or different from what is familiar to me:

1._____
2._____
3._____

Unlikely and Disaster Zones

I recommend that you merely acknowledge these zones. It is unwise to invest imagination into them.

Priorities operate within the larger context of our prosperity hierarchy. Being uncomfortably near a border of a familiar zone causes shifts in our priorities as we scramble to stay where we are comfortable. This exercise helps reveal priorities that are based on assumptions and fears.

Cultivating discipline on a national scale

Buddha said life is painful. It is the first of his Four Noble Truths. Buddha's recommended cure for pain is discipline. The dictionary says that discipline means to prepare by teaching. Properly done, that need not be unpleasant. Buddha said that discipline eventually eliminates pain. Embarking upon a program of discipline requires the vision to see past the short-term discomfort to the long-term result. We can identify the vision of an individual or a community by observing <u>what</u> they choose for the short and long term. The people of the United States lack a shared vision of the future. The job of leaders is to nurture, polish, and articulate a vision that appeals to people and represents a future that they want to work toward.

Once we understand our personal sense of time, we become more articulate citizens. We are able to comment with greater insight on the actions of our leaders and bureaucrats.

Too often politicians and business leaders emphasize their own job security and short term profitability over all else. This is destructive to the development of prosperity for the nation. That requires patience and continuity of effort. As citizens we must demonstrate a commitment to the long view and support leaders who do the same.

Warren Bennis, the preeminent authority on leadership today, writes, "the first leadership competency is the management of attention through a set of intentions or a vision, not in a mystical or religious sense, but in the sense of outcome, goal, or direction."[9] We tend to discourage such individuals as he describes from entering the political arena, largely because the arena has become so hostile and corrosive to human dignity. Few of us are willing to suffer the lies of a political opponent and then graciously serve him dinner in our home like my great grandfather Joseph did.

The large influx of immigrants we are witnessing marks a time when the collective vision of our nation must be reaffirmed. This can only be effective if the new arrivals are included in it. This is a challenging task that calls for courage and imagination on the part of leaders. It also requires enough eloquence to fire our imagination.

Eloquence comes in many forms including the simple folk wisdom of Harry Truman and the wit of Will Rogers.

Our national priorities show our confusion about the difference between now and later. Our national savings rate is too low. Our corporations strive to create short-term profit spikes to raise stock prices so that stockholders can play musical chairs to turn a quick buck. We are ready to spend $20,000 per year per prisoner, instead of getting to root causes that lead us to the world's second highest incarceration rate (after Russia), 14 times that of Japan. An article in *Worth* magazine in 1994 announced, "If you're looking for the investment of the future, think prisons." Private companies operate prisons in 17 states, and you can buy stock in the companies that run them. One financial analyst calls the investment "almost recession proof." Corrections Corporation of America declared in the early 1990s that it was well positioned, and they that expected the prison population to increase by hundreds of thousands. Their optimism has a macabre quality about it. Apart from the inhumanity of this approach, it is spectacularly expensive.

When it comes to priorities, actions speak louder than words. I argue in this book that we have plenty of money to pay down the federal deficit, a problem that hangs over our future like a loan shark's hit man waiting for us in the alley. We don't eliminate the deficit because doing so is not a high priority with the American people. We do not need to agree on all of our priorities in order to dissolve the deficit. We need only agree on that specific priority, and then work together in spite of our other differences.

Perhaps the biggest single problem facing the United States today is that we have lost the ability to move ahead in the face of diverse priorities. We have lost the ability to create alliances that survive long enough to bring people together for a specific, definable task. This sort of effort is called "ad hoc" in Latin. It means "for this specific purpose; for this case only." We have lost the ability to get together, in spite of disagreements, to do something we do agree on.

Former Representative Donald Pease, a Democrat from Ohio, was quoted in California's *Orange County Register* saying,

"Congress has no trouble acting when there is a clear public consensus ...the situation only gets worse when a powerful minority with strongly held views weighs in and thwarts a majority."[10] When the public agrees, Congress acts.

Our problem solving abilities have eroded to the point that mayors initiate lawsuits against their own state (LA's Riordan, for example), and states initiate lawsuits against the federal government (California's Wilson, for example), and citizens accept such abuses lying down.

We want to reduce the agony of AIDS, but we quarrel over how to do it rather than simply trying a lot of things to see what works best. The number of "official" AIDS cases reached 1,000,000 for the first time according to a World Health Organization (WHO) report published early in 1995. WHO estimates that the real number is 4,500,000. The difference is due to incomplete reporting and diagnosis. Some 19,500,000 individuals have acquired AIDS since the disease was identified.

How do we respond? Some people object to making sterile syringes available to drug addicts; others object to dispensing condoms to unmarried people, still more resist sex education in schools. While we quarrel over *methods*, the cost in both suffering and dollars runs rampant.

We either learn to form ad hoc work teams, or we will mire down in a morass of neglected problems. Elementary and high schools, so far as I know, place little or no emphasis on problem-solving, consensus building, or group communication skills. Developing leadership skills must become a primary focus of mainstream social institutions if we are to reorder our country in such a way that good government rises from the people.

Premise #4 of Wholistic Taxes:
Learning to work *ad hoc* is essential in a coherent society.

The priorities of this country are complex. It could not be otherwise among such a large and varied populace. The problem we face today is that our leaders are unskilled in weaving a fabric out of these many threads. The village elders too often abuse their privileges, and we are hungry for voices that speak the truth. In this vacuum, junk merchants step in and grab our attention. The senate filibuster is an example of junk communication. Television commercials that assume the viewer is simple minded are a form of junk that thrives because it has little competition. These problems yield in the presence of people with something worthwhile to say. These people are you and me.

Let us clarify our priorities in our personal lives and then declare our expectations at work and in Washington. This is what I understand by the phrase: "Let freedom ring."

Chapter Four: How to Pay Yourself First, and Why Many People Don't

I go to the party first, I play with my kids. I have Mark and Liza over for a party, we do the Easter egg hunt. I practice the piano, I'll paint a room, I'll trim the roses, I'll play with the dog, and then if there's nothing left to do, I'll even do the laundry. And when there's no laundry left, I'll take out the paper work, OK?
—Sharon Evans on tending to money issues

I know people who say they can't cook, and they live mostly on takeout food. I know a woman who prepares dinner no more than six times a year; fortunately for her she married a man who enjoys cooking. A lot of people operate their financial affairs with the same desire to distance themselves from the experience, usually because money intimidates them. They are "takeout" junkies. Their finances are, figuratively speaking, packed in styrofoam and are planned daily.

If you think that your financial situation is unmanageable, you might choose the common alternative of letting things seek their own level. People in this frame of mind ask themselves, "Gee, I wonder how this month will turn out?" Some people develop a lottery mentality, a hope that an unplanned windfall will erase all of life's financial problems in one glorious moment. That is not planning, that is wishing. Wishing is desire without action. We avoid actions that we think are too difficult for us. Fortunately, the action of managing money is easier when we are properly informed.

A feeling of incompetence with regard to money can derive from many sources. Women are often taught that money is beyond their understanding. Sons and daughters of rich parents may be intimidated by pressures, real or imagined, to compete with a performance they feel is beyond them.

I also see people avoid making money plans because they want to maintain a jaunty air of recklessness about them. There is a certain frontier bravado that these people like. There is no limit to the imaginative ideas that can be substituted for a sound financial plan. This book is for that time in your life when you are done with such substitutes.

While I speak in this book of a rational approach to money, I also acknowledge that few of us are rational about money. Thomas Moore says in *Care of the Soul* that money resists rational approaches. We must accept this paradox and work through it. Money is mysterious in much the same way that sex is mysterious. Money has aspects that are shadowy and confusing and often hypnotic in their appeal. We must face mystery if we are to enjoy life. The mysteries of life are the best parts! My advice is to approach the mystery of money with a blend of caution, curiosity, and a desire to be entertained.

It is important to preserve the awareness that this is an experience, so that you do not merge your sense of personal identity with money itself. People who look at their financial affairs and think they are seeing the reflection of their inner worth are supremely unhappy in their confusion. To think that increasing wealth simultaneously increases personal fulfillment leads to disappointment. If, however, we remain aware that money is a mystery to be experienced rather than something to own and dominate, we will have a largely positive encounter with it.

The word *appreciate* has largely been mistaken to mean *grateful*. The real meaning of appreciate is to be aware of the unique identity and value of something. To appreciate a painting means to recognize the effort and talent that was necessary to create it, and to have empathy with the artist in his or her struggle to access the vision needed to conceive of the image in the first place.

Appreciating something means we know what makes it special. We are discerning observers when we appreciate what we see.

We can achieve harmony with money by appreciating it. This means that we learn from our experiences with it. If we are short of money, we learn that the condition is a result of isolation and separation from the community of people. This isolation is something we experience as unemployment or underemployment. We tend to take this condition personally. Being without money may also mark a metaphorical winter in our lives, a time of barren fields and stillness and cold. It is possible to know our own winter even in the midst of friends who are busy harvesting the fields they have tended all summer.

When we have abundant money, we can learn to enjoy it without confusing that abundance with our own ego and its notions about itself. Appreciation is not fashionable in our times. We live in a time of polarization, a time of "either/or" thinking that discourages genuine appreciation. In order to become appreciative we must be willing to step aside from the crowd. Appreciation consists of noting differences without being judgmental and rejoicing in the uniqueness of things.

I recommend enjoying money itself apart from the amount of it that is accumulated.

If you are already comfortable with money management, and you are interested in expanding your knowledge of specific techniques and financial instruments, there are ample resources available to you. *Wholistic Taxes* does not attempt to add to your knowledge in that regard. Visit any book store or magazine stand, and you will see an abundance of advice in print. A constant stream of this material is necessary since the financial world is in a state of continuous change.

What is not so easy to find is the path through our fears and misconceptions to a clearing where we can recognize good advice and apply it. This is my reason for devoting a large portion of this book to counseling, and a lesser portion to discussions of specific techniques. To a person who has messy finances, a well-ordered, disciplined life often seems like the result of luck or special privilege. I like the definition of luck as "preparation meeting opportunity." If we are unprepared, luck is largely wasted on us anyway and we miss the opportunities. This book is intended to prepare you to be lucky.

Some people avoid planning a money strategy because they think money is bad, some kind of necessary evil. They endeavor to minimize the time they spend on this awful subject. I agree that money is mysterious. I agree that it is easy to become involved in compelling fantasies and delusions that center on money. It is tempting to use money to measure ourselves and our accomplishments, and to mistake its power as our own. All of these pitfalls are aspects of the mysteriousness of money. I do not think money is bad. I know that many people will not mention money in their prayers, including those prayers that include requests for other objects and experiences. For many people, money is tainted and not an appropriate subject for prayers. We may exclude it from conversation with friendly mortals too, and for the same reasons.

When money issues are embarrassing

We all want to avoid embarrassment. We have formally institutionalized our dislike of embarrassment. A tribal ritual ensures that we keep our remarks on a superficial level. You know this ritual, it goes like this: "How are you?" The reply of choice is, "I'm fine." You may not be fine, but you say you are. The other members of the tribe expect you to keep your concerns to yourself. Telling the truth would consume too much time.

Generally a person will sidestep an encounter with a potentially embarrassing question or situation. Since this strategy does not indicate courage or maturity, most of us will go the next step and cover up the evasion. We pretend that we stayed our original course and any perceived change was either coincidental or proper or both. As a final safeguard, we make a policy of not discussing such things. We evade, cover up the evasion, and forbid conversation about evasions and cover-ups in general lest the conversation turn our way and the light be directed at us. That combination of tactics usually produces a pretty airtight defense against embarrassment.

Having said that, most people are embarrassed about money. This puts my job of planning and filing taxes on a par with dentistry in terms of its appeal to some of my clients. People are reluctant to talk to one another about money, and they are reluctant to make plans where money is concerned. Let me say that even a sketchy plan is better than no plan at all. Any plan provides a reference point for change and improvement. Having no plan is the equivalent of empty space, or blank pages. It provides zero guidance. You have no way of knowing which action produced which result.

Experts who study organizational change have observed that inefficient companies consistently lack information about themselves. They are vague about work flow, routing of information and authority, job descriptions, and the organizational chart usually looks like a plate of spaghetti. Efficient companies, in contrast, have a large amount of information about themselves and their environment. Information is a root cause of change, and the warmer the welcome extended to information, the more easily change is implemented. This is true for companies and for individuals. The more you know about your finances, the more likely it is that you are at peace with money.

Death and taxes are certainties in our life; the main difference is we know when taxes are due. It is well to face death with our house in order. The same is true for taxes. With proper planning, you can avoid unpleasant surprises at tax time. I am such a strong advocate of tax planning that I apply the client's entire fee for initial tax planning to the charges for doing that year's tax return. This is to get the client thinking about the importance of tax planning.

What is money?

It is worth spending time to identify our notion of what money is. If we are going to make a plan to use it, we need some working model of what it might be. It might be helpful in our effort to put money in perspective to remember that pepper was used as money during the Middle Ages and as far back as classic Roman times. A pound of peppercorns was the equivalent of half a month's salary to a serf. At various times in history pepper could literally be traded for its weight in gold. Attila the Hun himself was placated with gifts, including pepper and cinnamon. Unlike pepper, paper currency is a symbol of wealth, not wealth itself.

Joseph Campbell, the famous mythologist and philosopher, said, "Money is congealed energy and releasing it releases life's possibilities." He went on to say, "Money experienced as life energy is indeed a meditation..."[11] Thomas Moore writes in *Care of the Soul* that money is "so filled with fantasy and emotion and resistant to rational guidance, that although it has much to offer, it can easily swamp the soul and carry consciousness off into compulsion and obsession." Accountants seldom use such language, but they are discussing the same topic. Accountants miss the dramatic themes that permeate the subject of money. They teach us details about housekeeping, but not the real meaning money represents. The wholistic approach to money recognizes the validity of both perspectives.

Attitudes determine saving habits

Money cannot be reduced to simple numbers on a page. Money touches us emotionally. Our handling of it speaks for our deepest beliefs and longings.

It is useful to identify what money "feels like." Does money, in the figurative sense, feel like sand to a kid in a sandbox? Do you throw it in the air to see if the wind will carry it? Does money feel precise and specific, a thing to be placed carefully and then watched? Until we know how money "feels" we do not understand our relationship with it and our expectations of it.

Those who are viewed as stingy often find comfort only when they are extremely orderly in their spending habits. It is the orderliness that they feel keeps them safe, so no matter how much money they have, they continue to handle it in an orderly way. Greed is not the same as extreme thrift. Greed is a reaction to something we want to avoid. The feverish pursuit of money is sometimes driven by a fear of poverty. Those who appreciate money are not driven to hoard it. The starting point for self-discovery is to identify the metaphor that describes the experiences you have when you handle money. Take a piece of paper and write, "When I have money come to me it feels like ..." Finish the sentence several times. Usually the first responses will be polite and practiced and quite dull. The revealing responses usually come only after several attempts.

When I was a teenager, one of my friends, Danny, never had money for small things, sodas, gum, candy, and so forth, but he was always the first one to get a new surfboard or bicycle. He was willing to be thought of as "cheap" on small items because larger items were his priorities.

For Dave, a devout Mormon, none of the reigning economic systems make sense. "I think they are all wrong," he says. "The only economic system I really believe in is the one God would have, and yet the world never really has." He believes the ideal system replaces the notion of ownership with stewardship. His system, he believes, eliminates extremes of poverty and wealth because the rich have no inclination to keep more than they need. Dave has nine children. His biggest personal extravagance is the occasional purchase of a book. He buys his clothes at the church thrift shop, and does so only when something falls apart and must be replaced.

Dave thinks society has become overly dependent on mass-produced goods and that self-sufficiency has fallen to a dangerously low level. He fears that the portion of the population that knows how to make useful things has grown perilously small while the number of sandwich makers and data entry clerks has mushroomed. He thinks this shift changes a stable societal pyramid into a column.

Dave's primary goal is "to not lose sight of that society, and whenever I can, to bring it about. I don't have any really hard ideas about how I am going to do that, but just to be ready, and this is a religious thing. The leaders will make us aware of the need to make ourselves self-sufficient as a people."

One wonderful lady I served died in 1985 at the age of 80. For the last decade of her life she supported herself entirely from her Social Security check, which was about $600 each month. The odd thing about this woman was that she had a monthly income of more than $10,000 and an estate valued in excess of $3,000,000. She had lived through the depression and came out of it with an overwhelming compulsion to save money. When she passed away, her heirs immediately went about enjoying her money. They had no memory of the depression and thought their relative's way of life was strange.

Our point of view about money shapes our experiences with it. It is informative to identify the metaphors that describe our experience of money and the physical sensations that we associate with money. These steps help in that discovery. My prescription involves two treatments:

❑   Recognize that money is more than record keeping and decision making. It is an emotionally-charged and mysterious aspect of life.

❑   If money management is a problem for you, the solution is to get beyond collecting knowledge about bookkeeping and budgeting issues and explore the nature and origins of your beliefs about money.

For many people this includes the way they handle credit card debt, which may create a nagging feeling of being fiscally irresponsible. When you identify habits that hold you back from going in the direction that appeals to you, you can't rest until you get your freedom.

If you find yourself experiencing great discomfort over the way you handle money, one of two things is happening. You are trying to live in step with someone else's value system and it conflicts with your own in painful ways, or you are operating with too little information and getting too little a return on your efforts and time. The latter problem is the equivalent of stubbing your toes in a dark room. The remedy is more knowledge and self-understanding.

If you are compulsive about spending, your problem may not

be money focused at all. Money management is more likely a symptom of a broader concern. I recommend exploring your views in a comprehensive way using books by John Bradshaw and Deepak Chopra for insights to guide you to an understanding of what moves you. See the bibliography for specific suggestions.

For many of us, the murkiness of money as an issue in our lives is complicated by a concern that we might be greedy and that being greedy is bad. Webster's Dictionary defines greed as "excessive desire for acquiring or having; desire for more than one needs or deserves." This definition of greed works better for me: Greed is the compulsive pursuit of the opposite of what you want to avoid.

> **Premise #5 of Wholistic Taxes:**
> **Money is more than numbers on a page.**

Consider your savings account to be a bill

Having examined some of the ways we mistake money as a measure of ourselves, let's turn to some practical ways to place ourselves at the top of our own priority list. Start with saving money. It is essential to treat savings as though it is a bill. The reason is that savings must have the same compelling quality as the bills. The squeaky wheel, the greater urgency, will always get our attention. This trait is hard-wired into our nervous system from many years of evolution. We do the most urgent things first in order to survive. Make saving urgent.

You can make savings seem more urgent by reminding yourself that the car *will* need repairs. Someone you love *will* invite you to attend their wedding 2,000 miles away. Countless other things will happen that will cost money. These are bills in the same compelling sense of the word as the bills sitting on your desk waiting for you to write a check. You might as well set money aside to pay them now because their arrival is a certainty.

The amount of savings I recommend is ten percent of your

take home pay. When your income is large, it makes sense to expand this amount because your basic needs are met with much less than 90 percent of your income. If you cannot, or think you cannot manage ten percent, set any amount you want. The point is to establish a consistent habit of saving something, and increase it when you can.

If you are in debt more than you would like to be, I recommend concentrating your efforts to retire your debt. Start with simple things, then move to more ambitious tactics later. The most basic steps are:

❑ Stop adding debt.

❑ Pay cash, or do without.

❑ Pay off the most expensive debt first, the one with the highest interest rate.

❑ Save *something* even though most of your money may be going to retire debts.

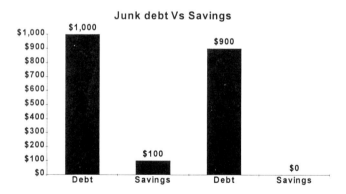

If you have an extra $100 it is better to start a savings account than to apply it against a debt. The two illustrations above show how this works. Rather than reducing a $1,000 debt by 10 percent, start saving. There are two important reasons for this. First, you will have cash for genuine emergencies. Second, you will install an important habit, the habit of saving money. Once you have established a base of good habits, you are ready for more ambitious ways to pay yourself first. The following list addresses some of the most common methods.

The term *junk debt* refers to debts for perishables, which means everything that has no cash value after its purchase. This includes items such as clothes, restaurant meals, and countless other purchases. These are often the impulse purchases that are properly postponed until they can be made with cash.

What to do with a raise

Whether or not you like income taxes, there is a valuable lesson you can learn from them. The lesson is the simple device of the graduated scale of percentages. Simply stated, the more you make, the more you pay. You can also take the position that the more you make, the more you will save. As your income increases, you can move to a higher percentage savings rate according to a scale that you define in advance.

If you determine that your present income permits you to save 5 percent of your gross income, you might decide to increase that to 7.5 percent of your new income after getting a raise. If your income varies, perhaps due to commissions, you might decide to save 5 percent of a fixed amount and 10 percent of the excess beyond that amount. The complexity of your formula can be adapted infinitely to your personal preferences so that the "fit" is right for you. A good fit increases the probability that you will stay with the graduated savings plan. Besides the cash you accumulate, you will also experience a feeling of satisfaction as your savings grow. It is a natural high. Try it! You'll like it!

Mortgage games

For most people, their mortgage is their biggest single expense, and a mortgage typically gobbles up a tremendous amount of money in the form of interest. One of my clients lives in a condominium in Huntington Beach. The principal portion of his mortgage payment is currently around $133.00 per month. Almost twelve hundred dollars more goes for interest. He has decided that each month he will make an overpayment amount equal to the amount of principal paid that month. Why this amount? It struck him as achievable and a fun way to hack at that big clod of debt. He likes the fact that the overpayment will increase gradually, as he expects his income to do. There is nothing wrong with doing whatever strikes you as amusing, clever, or enjoyable in the game of whittling down debt.

Another useful technique is to continue to pay the old, higher amount after refinancing at a lower interest rate. If the old amount was affordable, why not continue it and retire the loan that much sooner?

Bucket savings

Another way to fine-tune your savings plan is to have sub-accounts for specific uses. These sub-accounts might be called buckets. You might literally put the money in envelopes, or you might keep it all in the bank if you are careful enough with your bookkeeping. The bucket plan is especially useful for lump-sum payments that come in cycles. Insurance premiums and property tax payments are typical examples of such expenses. It is much easier to pay these bills if you save for them each month.

Tom Peters, the man who popularized the principles of Total Quality Management, said, "What gets measured gets done." It applies equally in business and in personal life. One of the most useful things we can do is set goals and measure our progress toward them.

One of the characteristics of government is to borrow money for repairs and improvements. In a well-run condominium complex, reserves are maintained in the "bucket savings" format for major maintenance items such as street surfacing, roofs, painting, pool restoration, and the like. The private organization measures what it has and how quickly it is accumulating money to make replacements when they are needed. This sort of measurement works better than the government's management-by-crisis approach. I recommend measuring what you have and your progress toward your goals.

Saving with professional help

It is always wise to have a financial planner assist you because this person will see you operating on auto pilot and will point it out to you. If you are caught in a habit, you probably repeat it unconsciously. An advisor will break your decision making process down into steps so that you can examine each one. Each step is a decision point.

People have a tendency to think they should wait until their affairs are more together, or they have more money to invest. This is like stalling the maid until you have cleaned up the worst of the mess around the house. Some advisors do specialize or limit their practice to big league investors, but there are plenty of them who welcome all clients, so don't be put off by fears of not being ready for advice. When you choose an advisor do the following:

- ❏ Pick one who is as friendly as you are.
- ❏ Ask questions freely.
- ❏ Test the advice you get the old fashioned way. Does it make sense?
- ❏ Be aggressive in the face of strange terms or financial double talk.

Fancy inventions like "derivatives" and junk bonds usually fall into disrepute sooner or later. Some derivatives, in the words of the *Orange County Register*, "are so wildly esoteric that only the most sophisticated professionals armed with high-powered computer programs can keep track of them."[12] If a plan is too complicated for you to understand, it may simply be too gimmicky. Why assume that the confusion is your fault? Get a second opinion on anything that makes you uneasy, whether it is on the grounds of logic or intuition. There have been many blunders in the financial community. No one ought to be treated as a sacred cow.

The importance of a second opinion

Theodore Leavitt points out in his classic book, *The Marketing Imagination*, that once a person succeeds at something he is inclined to think that the way he did it is the way you must do it if you want the same result. He writes, "Practitioners, filled with pride and money, turn themselves into prescriptive philosophers, filled mostly with hot air." The good professor does not ignore his own specialty. He says professors turn into consultants "filled mostly with woolly congestion." If you have met a rich, proud fellow to whom you give money in exchange for advice, you may still need a second opinion. His, or hers, may be mostly hot air.

A second opinion means two things. First, it means getting an opinion other than your own. While this may seem obvious, it isn't always. Financial planners are the specialists to consult in this area. My friend Dion Collins, a certified financial planner, tells of clients who came to see him in year six of their twenty years of lottery payments. They had been advising themselves, and discovered that they had almost nothing to show for the half million dollars that had passed through their hands. They decided to get a second opinion.

There is no need to pick on the lottery winners. Most people lack a plan for their financial future. For many, it is easier to talk about sex than about money. Most people embark on financial planning with a nagging sense that something is wrong and no clear idea about how to set it right. That is a good reason to get help.

The best way to choose an advisor is to begin with a class on the subject in which you want advice. These are likely to be offered at colleges in your area. This approach enables you to learn the terminology of your chosen subject and to identify the sub-specialties that categorize the experts available to you. It also puts you in a learning environment where you probably won't be subject to someone with his own agenda working to recruit you as a client. At least it is likely to be a mild sales pitch.

After this basic orientation, the next step is likely to be a recommendation from someone you already know. A friend, or your CPA, will probably be able to recommend a financial planner who will take good care of you. You might ask your financial planner to recommend a CPA. Almost all of my clients are referred to me, and that is true for the majority of people for whom I have the greatest respect.

Shocking though it sounds, not all advisors are honest. Our trade organization, the AICPA, investigated 634 members of our trade for misconduct, including tax violations, in 1993. When it comes to tax preparation, be wary. There is little regulation in this area. There is currently no minimum age, although the IRS is currently considering a requirement that anyone who takes money for preparing another person's return must be at least 18 years old.

Investment advice from independent advisors (those who do not work for an investment house) is likely to be less influenced by pressures to sell the house brand of investment products. The important credentials to look for are certification and registration. A Certified Financial Planner is well educated by virtue of completing the certification course. A registered financial planner is accountable to the Securities and Exchange Commission, which serves as a watchdog over him or her. In California, the Department of Corporations also has authority over registered planners.

Planners have different ways of charging for their services. They may receive commissions. Two advantages of commissions include the fact that the ticking clock incurs no fees and that the commission-driven advisor is likely to have a thorough knowledge of the financial products that are available. You only pay when you buy something, so he wants to be well informed. The downside is that commissions may influence the advisor's choice of recommendations, and investments with higher risks often pay higher commissions.

They may work on an hourly rate, or they might charge a flat fee that is some percentage of the amount being managed. The obvious advantage here is that commissions don't influence their choices (provided you know if they are getting commissions). A potential disadvantage is that the advisor may be less alert to the products in a market place.

One interesting method that appeals to me is the fee-offset method. Under this arrangement the client pays an hourly rate, and if she purchases a product that pays the advisor a commission, the commission amount is applied to the hourly. It offsets the fee, hence the name fee-offset. This saves the client the effort of making the purchase elsewhere while simultaneously eliminating the advisor's temptation to sell products because they pay a commission rather than because they serve the client's best interests.

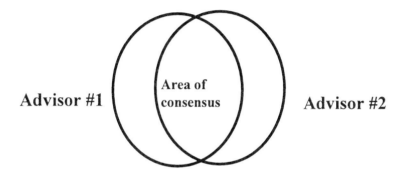

If the advice you receive makes you feel uncomfortable, I suggest that you seek a second opinion. The area where both advisors agree is likely to be the safest path.

You can get a certain amount of information simply by asking. If you sense that your advisor may be profiting from you in ways that go beyond your direct payment of fees, ask. If he is keen on you buying something specific, he must tell you if he is getting a commission on the sale, so just ask. A CPA is forbidden by law to accept commissions, but other accountants can get them. You might find an accountant representing a limited partnership, and his advice on the partnership might be suspect while he is wearing his accounting hat.

For a second opinion on the advice you get, it is usually best to get an opinion from a second expert. Consider the illustration on this page. It represents how the opinions of two people might overlap. The circles represent of the points of view and opinions of two advisors. The circles might overlap more than these in the drawing, but they illustrate the principle. The overlapping area defines the range of consensus. The safest area is the common ground. Because of the inevitable disparity in the areas of agreement, it is important to be an <u>active participant</u> in the decision-making.

To review, the steps to saving money are:

- ❑ Examine your attitudes and assumptions about money.
- ❑ Identify those things that you do automatically.
- ❑ Start with the issues that face you *today*.
- ❑ Play mortgage games,
- ❑ Adopt bucket savings,
- ❑ Pay off high interest debts first.
- ❑ Get professional advice sooner rather than later.

Everyone can achieve security and peace of mind about money.

Chapter Five: An Overview of Investments and Risk

The hardest thing in the world to understand is the income tax.

—Albert Einstein

W hat is risk? What is the relationship between risk and prosperity? You might want to set this book down for a moment to think about what risk means to you. Consider what taking or avoiding risks indicates to you about a person. Our desire to avoid risk, scientists tell us, is part of our evolutionary heritage. Our modern human brain is wrapped around a smaller portion, the "old" brain, that we have in common with less intelligent animals. This "lizard brain" is the part of the brain that limits its choices to fleeing or fighting. The part of the brain unique to us humans, the "new" brain, can choose among more subtle and more elegant choices such as negotiation and compromise. As human beings, we are still learning to define and assess risk.

Recent studies have shown that, on average, risk taking does not improve performance among investors in the financial markets. Naturally, there are exceptions. There is always the story of the long shot that paid off. If you have plenty of money, putting part of it on long shots can be fun and profitable, but I don't consider it an investment.

Long shots come in three forms. The first is gambling, and in that area I must leave you to your own devices. The second is that personal Opus which your Muse compels you to pursue whether it is strictly logical or not. This book is part of my Opus. If it provides a profit, it does so against the odds. On the other hand, if it does not provide a profit, no real harm is done to my financial situation.

The third form is the promising new venture, or the chance that a declining company will get a second wind.

When it comes to investing, however, neither long shots nor high risks have a place. Solid research justifies this conclusion. Studies show that bonds and mutual funds that are managed conservatively tend to do as well as the market in general. Gregory Millman, writing in *Worth* magazine observed, "In one study only 15 of 121 funds beat the index. Those that did took less risk than the index. The poor performers took more risk." He was speaking of bond funds, but the magazine said much the same thing about mutual funds in the previous issue.

Bonds can be quite exotic. Former Orange County Treasurer Robert Citron speculated with public money by investing in exotic derivatives such as "inverse floaters." The very name should send you running for cover. Not only did he invest badly, he did it with borrowed money. You could hardly ask for a more grandiose example of what not to do. Is private industry smarter? Proctor & Gamble lost $102,000,000 on derivatives in 1994. It seems that if you give something a fancy enough name, and make it expensive, somebody will buy it. It is interesting that the big Wall Street firms gave the Orange County investment portfolio a checkup and said there were "no major concerns." Later the $2,000,000,000 loss was all over the front page.

"Too good to be true" schemes probably are, but they still trap many unwary investors from alleged experts like Citron to ordinary folks in the street. It is important to get an impartial, objective opinion from somebody who does not stand to profit by your purchase.

A series of bogus investments was profiled on a recent television special. In one instance the investor was content with assurances from the perpetrator of the hoax that his money was safe. A second opinion would have likely prevented the loss he suffered of money that came from a settlement resulting from the wrongful death of his mother. I suggest extreme caution with any investment that offers more than double passbook savings rates. In the story I am referring to, the investor was told to expect 10 percent per <u>month</u>. The hoax was so extreme that it would have been obvious to any reliable advisor.

I encourage you to put aside the notion that risk is necessary to achieving substantial gains through your investments. Instead of seeking home runs, I recommend concentrating on base hits. Get a runner on first base. Let subsequent batters drive earlier runners home.

You will probably be somewhere to the left of the positions I take on various issues such as assessing risks when it comes to investing money. Being conservative is a good trait for a CPA, or in any event I make the best of it that I can. I'm too conservative for the average person. For years after I could afford new cars, I only bought used cars. I did this because the cost of ownership the first year in terms of depreciation is distressingly high for the kind of cars I like.

These figures are based on 1993 models. The $66, 828 Corvette will cost you $24,000 in depreciation the first year! If you drive 12,000 miles per year, your cost is $2.00 per mile in lost value before you buy gas or insurance! The sturdy Lexus, in comparison, drops from $40,130 to $37,500 in the first year. This translates to 22 cents per mile in depreciation. The Japanese car loses 6.5 percent of its show room price in a year, the 'Vette loses a staggering 36 percent. The Jeep Cherokee, so fashionable with the thirty-something crowd, hovers somewhere in the middle with a 13 percent decline in price the first year.

We are not discussing which car to buy, I just wanted to put my preferences into perspective. You can judge my advice based on how different your temperament is from mine, adding as many grains of salt to each suggestion as is appropriate for you. Let's quickly review the various kinds of investments available to you.

As you survey these, bear in mind the six investment factors that help you determine which investment is most appropriate for you.

They are:

- ❑ Risk
- ❑ Liquidity
- ❑ Taxability
- ❑ Growth
- ❑ Income
- ❑ Ease of management.

Ease of management focuses on the trade off between time and money. I have clients who found that their investments grew to a level of complexity that kept them busy beyond their idea of what retirement was meant to be. I usually advise clients in this situation to hire a portfolio manager. A portfolio big enough to impose seriously on your schedule ought to be profitable enough to pay for the attention of a professional manager and still yield sufficient income to the owner.

A simple way to compare estimates

Comparing a number of prospective investments is easier when you assign point values to each of the criteria listed above. You can award each characteristic from zero to four points to determine which investment is more attractive given your needs and preferences. The investment with the highest number of points is the most logical one.

This assumes that you are not making investment decisions based on emotional considerations. My experience corresponds with that of other financial professionals: women are less willing to take risks than men. Women often show less self-confidence with money in general. The following chart will therefore be read differently based on gender. I encourage women to see past any conditioning that has been imposed upon them due to their gender. Women are fully as capable as men when it comes to money.

There is no perfect investment, and a balanced portfolio will result in a combination of risk and return that is appropriate for you and your situation.

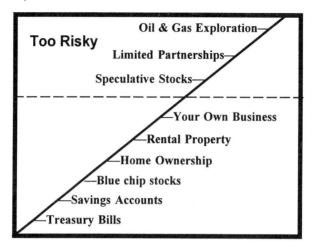

This chart shows the relative risks of different investments. When all is said and done, remember that money is a replaceable commodity.

Investment number 1: treasury bills

One of the safest investments is treasury bills (T-bills). Treasury bills, notes, and bonds are distinguished by the length of their maturation period: bills (less than two years), notes (two to ten years), bonds (longer than ten years). The government also issues savings bonds which can be cashed at any point in time (although with interest penalties), and which pay interest from issue date to redemption date. These investments are safe because they are guaranteed by the federal government. When the government runs out of money it prints more. The downside of this investment is that T-bills typically have a low interest rate. As I write this, passbook savings rates of two to three percent make T-bills look fairly robust. By investing in T-bills you generally give up yield in return for security.

Municipal bonds have historically been considered one of the safest investments. The Orange County, California bankruptcy is a high-profile example of how unreliable traditional wisdom can be. Increasingly, it is the responsibility of the investor to ask questions. Questions that might once have been considered dumb are not dumb at all. The disaster County Tax Collector Bob Citron created was made possible by the fact that his peers and colleagues were reluctant to ask penetrating questions. It would be better for all of us had they asked "dumb" questions of this alleged expert.

Investment number 2: savings accounts

Savings accounts are safe and dull. They are the private sector equivalent of treasury bills. They are insured to $100,000 by the FDIC (in the case of banks) or by the FSLIC (in the case of savings & loans). The financial institutions tell you that you can have multiple accounts with different names on them so that each is insured to $100,000. While this is true, it is even safer when you have more than $100,000 in savings accounts to deposit it to different banks. This eliminates the chance of a clerical error combining your funds under one account or name so that the $100,000 limit applies. The other consideration is that banks fail, Beverly Hills Savings & Loan and Palos Verdes National Bank being conspicuous examples in southern California. So far, the government has not failed.

Investment number 3: blue-chip stocks

Blue-chip stocks are stocks which are deemed relatively safe by virtue of their proven track record. Typically, blue-chip companies have already experienced their period of exponential growth and settled into a predictable pattern of maturity. You missed their "sky rocket" period, they are showing a little gray hair, and they are considered reliable. While they will not double in price overnight, they are unlikely to go down to zero overnight either. The traditional reasons for investing in blue-chip stocks include a steady income stream from dividends and the potential increase in price per share. Another reason is that your friends will be more impressed hearing about your investments in prestigious companies that are known to them as compared to your investment in a robot-driven widget factory being built in Micronesia to supply the growing demand for widgets in Argentina.

The chart includes two categories of stock: blue-chip and speculative. Speculative stocks can produce exponential growth, but nearly always with a corresponding increase in risk. It is fun to tell tales of buying Apple at $10, but it is a game to be played only with discretionary funds, not with your retirement nest egg. In 1992, IBM, one of the most famous blue-chip stocks, dropped from around $150 per share to around $50 per share after falling for less than a year. This drastic drop in price caused a reduction in the net worth of the owners of the stock. Even more devastating, however, was the drop in dividends which caused stockholders' incomes to drop. Combined with the drop in price, it hurt the investors two ways.

The slippery footing that plagues even the blue chip companies argues for investing in a blue-chip mutual fund instead of a specific stock. The risk chart does not list mutual funds because they vary widely in character and cover the entire range of risk. Mutual funds pool your money with that of other investors and spread it over a number of investments. This softens the blow of individual unpleasant surprises that may come from any given stock. There are approximately 5,000 mutual funds today, which is about ten times more than in 1980. There are now more mutual funds than there are publicly traded stocks on the NYSE. One mutual fund varies from another primarily in the combination of stocks it includes.

Choosing a mutual fund is no easier than choosing an individual stock. In some ways it is more difficult since the fund doesn't "make" anything that you can examine and study. With a stock, you are buying into a manufacturing plant or a shipping line or a utility or something else that is tangible to some degree. With mutual funds you are buying into the judgment of somebody who makes decisions for you.

Studies show that mutual funds, on average, do about the same as the stock market in general. With thousands of mutual funds, there are bound to be some extreme examples at both ends of the spectrum, and there are. Some funds invest in the growing segments of the stock market and do conspicuously better than average for a while, but taken as a whole, all a mutual fund does is spread your risk over a broad base of stocks. Mutual funds are best seen as a vehicle for common sense investing, not as a variation on the lottery.

Mutual funds specialize in the sort of investments they make. Some invest globally. Some seek out small companies with perceived potential for growth; others look for mature companies that are mending old injuries or about to move to a new plateau for some other reason. It is important to understand the overall intention of the mutual fund you choose for your investment.

It is a good idea to wait until a fund is five years old before you invest in it. This gives it time to prove itself. You can also be fairly sure that a fund will settle in value after the initial sale. If you buy at ten, it will probably go to nine as soon as the dust settles from the early buying enthusiasm. You can generally wait a few months to a year and buy at nine. The same is true for initial public offerings, or IPOs as they are called. In the first nine months of 1993, 1,765 domestic companies went public. By November 831, or 47 percent of them, were selling for less than their initial price. The initial fall triggers more sales for a variety of reasons, and good businesses that are likely to do well are suddenly marked down.

I recommend against buying a "house brand" mutual fund. If you want to change to another investment house, they will not represent "brand x" for you. You have to sell the fund (which is a taxable event) and take your cash to your new advisor and buy her brand. Better to buy one that all brokers can handle for you.

Investment number 4: your own home.

> *With wheat you will always be able to get the gold; but with gold you may not always be able to get the wheat. The time is fast approaching when the owners of the land will be the rulers of the world. Actual ownership of the soil, and the development of its resources, form the basis of all wealth. Why not become the owner of some, TODAY? Not tomorrow.*
>
> *—Promontory-Curlew Land Company, Logan, Utah, advertisement, 1915.*

I live in southern California. From the end of World War II to 1989, real estate values here increased consistently, with only minor reductions, and a lot of people were making more money from their home's appreciation than from their jobs. From 1986 to 1990 Los Angeles homes increased in price from an average of $96 per square foot to $157 per square foot. So why list homes so far up the risk slope in the chart? One reason is that the boom has ended, at least for now, and a lot of people have been caught in a squeeze resulting from lost jobs and the burden of an inflated mortgage. The result: an avalanche of foreclosures.

In the popular community of Thousand Oaks, north of Los Angeles, homes smaller than 2,500 square feet lost a quarter of their value from 1989 to 1994. Larger houses in the same locale dropped more than 50%. Foreclosures, nearly 24,000 of them in Los Angeles County alone in 1993, double the number during the recession of 1983, are the main cause. Each foreclosure becomes a "comp" which lowers the price of the next sale, and the downward spiral is seemingly endless.[13] Realtors estimated that one home in four sold in 1994 might have been in foreclosure. In Beverly Hills prices have returned to levels of 1985. As one realtor said, "Today, in Beverly Hills, $1 million will give you a myriad of choices."[15]

What nobody noticed during the home pricing boom in Southern California was that the jobs started leaving town— 524,000 of them in five years. These jobs were the good jobs like engineering posts at McDonnell Douglas, and management jobs at General Motors. The growing employment sectors were clerical and janitorial. You cannot support a $260,000 mortgage making sandwiches at McDonald's.

Does this affect taxes? Of course it does. In Los Angeles County the real estate tax base declined $5,800,000,000 in 1993 alone, or an average of 11 percent overall. It will decline more as homes with inflated prices continue to sell at deflated prices in bankruptcy and foreclosure proceedings.

Another reason to consider homes a relatively high-risk investment is the lack of liquidity. If you need to sell your home, it is difficult to do it today and get your money tomorrow. While it

77

varies with current market conditions, it typically takes three months to a year to sell a house. In a declining market every month costs money. The incentive for trading up today is that you take a smaller loss on the house you are leaving in exchange for the seller taking a larger loss on the home you are acquiring. He who loses least, wins.

A house is a sensible investment because you need a place to live. It makes sense to buy a home and build up equity. The tax benefits of owning your own home include being able to itemize mortgage interest and property taxes as deductions. Improvements to your property increase its value, and provide enjoyment as well. Selling costs are quite high with real estate compared to the transaction costs of selling other investments. Selling expenses could eat up some or all of the appreciation on your property.

There is a great deal of bad advice going around about mortgage interest. It is presented as useful and desirable.

The pie charts in chapter three show how to reduce your net worth. You buy something you don't want because the money spent is deductible. It reduces your taxable income. You spend $1.00 and you get back 35 cents from Uncle Sam. The deductibility of mortgage interest can fool us into thinking it is a good thing. The following table shows why it doesn't make sense.

Mortgage Interest	Tax Savings 35%	Net Cost Out of Pocket
1) $1,200	$420	$780
2) $1,000	$350	$650

In scenario #1 you pay $1,200 in mortgage interest and save $420 in taxes. In scenario #2 you pay $1,000 in mortgage interest and save "only" $350 in taxes. #1 saves you $70 more than #2, but you had to spend $200 to save $70, so your net worth was $130 lower with a $1,200 mortgage interest expense than with a $1,000 expense. Take a moment to review this example. It is not difficult, but it may be a totally new concept to you, as it is to many of my clients.

Mortgage interest is an example of a financial device that is a complete waste of money. Add to that the high fees someone will charge you to render that bad advice to prolong your mortgage payments, and you begin to appreciate the phrase, "adding insult to injury." Right now some accountant is giving out this advice and charging for it. Can you hear it? The advisor looks longingly at the equity in his client's home and says, "You need write-offs. Keep your mortgage. Or, why not borrow against your equity?" My response is: What investment is better, safer, and provides more peace of mind than your own home?

What do you get when you pay mortgage interest? Nothing. The rationale for paying mortgage interest is that Uncle Sam didn't get your money. That is true, but neither did you.

When you keep your money, or spend it on something you want and which adds to your net worth, you keep 65 cents and you send 35 cents to your Uncle. I deem this the superior strategy.

> **Premise #6 of Wholistic Taxes:**
> **Spend to build net worth, not to reduce taxes.**

Financial planners usually encourage clients to live with their mortgages. This generally leaves more ready cash available to act on the advisor's advice. (I happily know two exceptions, financial advisors who really look out for their clients in this regard. They are Lisa Chapman, who is with PaineWebber, and Dion Collins, who owns Dion Collins Advisory. Both are certified financial planners, which means they passed a comprehensive series of exams to earn the certificate.)

The days of buying a home as a speculative investment over, at least for now. People are buying homes with their heads, not out of ambition. They are buying homes that are already in good shape because, on average, they don't have additional money to fix them up. Home buying still remains out of reach for many in our society. In Los Angeles, just 36 percent of households have the money to buy a home.

Housing costs vary dramatically with location. Ernst & Young analyzes housing costs annually. Their 1994 report showed that Houston is the most affordable housing market. Residents there, on average, pay 18.5 percent of the household income for housing. Honolulu residents, according to the survey, pay a whopping 56.5 percent of their income for housing. Los Angeles ranked 68th in affordability with a 41.5 percent share going for housing. This regional disparity of share-of-income needed for housing is one more reason why one budget can't fit all people.

I recommend buying in the best neighborhood you can afford, not the best house. This is likely to put you in one of the "humbler" homes in the neighborhood you choose. The reason for this is that the financial stability of your neighbors is a form of protection for your investment. Improvements you make to your home are more likely to recoup their cost should you decide to sell. In a neighborhood where your home stands out, your improvements are likely to exceed the neighborhood, and you may not find a buyer who will pay for what you have done.

It is always wise to examine home improvements closely if your intention is to increase your home's value, as distinct from increasing the pleasure of living in it. A study by *Remodeling* magazine revealed that the impact of a remodel varies not only with the project chosen, but with the region of the country. A new bathroom adds more value in San Francisco than in Sioux Falls. This difference applies to both absolute dollar costs and as a percentage. If your improvements are viewed as an investment for resale purposes, do your homework thoroughly. Your local realtor is an excellent source of advice. If the improvements are merely intended to please you, and you don't care so much about getting your money back, the decision is simpler.

It is worth noting that raising money by raiding an IRA or other tax-deferred fund is an extremely expensive source of funds. It costs an average of 50 percent to pull money out of these sources prematurely. Avoid doing so if at all possible. It is better to borrow from parents. I have found that parents who have the money are generally receptive to such loans provided that the borrowers can demonstrate a workable plan to pay it back.

Some of the most devastating mistakes I have seen involve real estate investments. Parents of a friend of mine wanted to live near the ocean. They traveled extensively and arrived in Savannah, Georgia on its good day. They paid cash for a piece of property. Two weeks later the mosquitoes were so bad they walked away from it. Five years later they still haven't sold it, even after reducing the price by 50 percent. They have since bought a piece of property in Oregon, but they have so much cash tied up in Georgia that they cannot build their dream home as they intended.

Another couple I know moved to a rustic home in Oregon. There they learned why Oregon is so green, and they developed an intense dislike for big, gray clouds and the oppressive damp cold that characterizes Oregon weather. After a couple of years of trying, they discovered that they could not sell their home and its 40 acres. Even if they had, California real estate had exploded in value, a phenomenon that made lots of people better off during the late 1980s, at least on paper. As a result, they could not afford to reenter the quality of home they had sold.

My suggestion for avoiding these disappointments is to research the location thoroughly. If you can't decide based on facts alone, rent a place that will provide the experience of living there without a binding commitment. A few months' rent is the better investment in comparison to owning a home you don't want and that you may have problems selling.

Investment number 5: rental real estate.

You might remember the heyday of the real estate evangelists and their message of get-rich-quick-without-cash. Like most clever schemes, there was a kernel of truth at the bottom of this one. There was a time when some of those devices worked. If you followed these preachers too late in the game, however, they could drag you into bankruptcy. Housing prices have stalled and declined since 1989, and real estate speculation is not a rewarding game at present. Things that seem too good to be true, things like the "nothing-down" crowd taught, may work briefly, but they are usually a fluke. I recommend wariness of all get-rich-quick schemes.

Real estate is basically an illiquid investment. Rental property has the appealing advantage that someone else, provided that person is reliable, makes the payments. There are important tax advantages with rental real estate. (Schedule E is used to report income and expenses from rental real estate.) The primary exposure to risk is that someone else, your tenant, has control of your asset.

The biggest downside of rental property as an investment may be the burden of management. Rental property may require a large amount of hands-on attention. I have a client who complains to me that he spends four or five hours a day managing his rental properties and his stock portfolio. It is possible to hire someone to manage investments on a commission basis, and this trade-off can restore free time to the retired individual, and management fees are tax deductible, so the net cost is 65 percent after taxes.

The table below is useful in assessing your appetite for risk. It presents a context-free offering of how you might choose to invest $100,000. Context-free means that it excludes questions such as local occupancy rates and other related information that you would use in a complete examination of your options. Given the absence of a context, which approach best suits your appetite for risk?

# of properties	% down	Equity	Mortgage
1	100%	$100K	0
2	50%	$100K	$100K
5	20%	$100K	$400K
10	10%	$100K	$900K

The more properties you own, the more susceptible you are to changes in real estate values. Your response to the six investment factors (risk, liquidity, taxability, growth, income, and ease of management) have a bearing on how many properties are right for you to buy.

Investment number 6: your own business

According to statistics, for those of you who trust them, approximately 80 percent of new businesses fail in the first five years. Those of you who don't trust statistics will quickly poke holes in this number. Many members in this group of "failures" are in fact acquired or merged with bigger companies, or are closed voluntarily after a profitable experience for the owner. Entrepreneurs gain valuable experience running their independent shops, and some companies use this talent pool to refresh their work force. Statistically this produces "failed" enterprises as operators close up shop to graze in greener pastures to which their sharpened skills give them access.

Even taking these failures at face value, the outlook is not all that bad. If 20 percent of the new corporations formed in 1993 are still operating in 2001, that will enlarge the business community by 147,000 businesses. On a cumulative basis that order of growth is substantial. This number only counts corporations. Add to that sole proprietorships and partnerships, and the numbers are truly invigorating.

Some industries are notorious for producing high failure rates. These include manufacturing, retail, and restaurants. This is because of high start-up costs for equipment and inventory. Another reason is that restaurants lose a significant amount of inventory to spoilage. Businesses which are less susceptible to failure include service businesses which can be started with minimal capital.

Entrepreneurs are frequently described as risk-takers, with the innuendo added that entrepreneurs enjoy risks. Perhaps some do, but it has been my experience that entrepreneurs like their businesses to be as safe and predictable as possible. They get their thrills on the ski slopes or in some other activity where the risks are narrowly defined, not by deliberately seeking them in a business context. What they do that is often mistaken for risk taking is really a matter of facing their fears. Entrepreneurs must face their fears. People in a corporate environment might be able to avoid that task, or at least get less deeply into it. Those who establish their own businesses cannot. This willingness to face fear and move ahead anyway might seem headlong and reckless to others, but it seldom indicates thrill seeking for its own sake, as far as I have seen.

In spite of the risks, the allure of the many good reasons for starting a business brings many people into the fray each year. These include being the boss, the opportunity for enjoying the profits rather than passing them on, flexibility of hours, and many other reasons unique to each individual's tastes. The downside of owning your own business may include long hours, the need to master a wide variety of skills such as sales, marketing, and bookkeeping, the emotional pressures, and the fear of failure.

The prospect of becoming an entrepreneur raises the question of whether you prefer to be a big fish in a small pond, or a small fish in a big pond. Launching out on your own creates a paradox. You are a big fish in the sense of being in charge of the business you own, but your company itself may be a small fish in the ocean of commerce. Compare this to your situation in a corporate environment where you might be a small cog on one of many wheels. On the other hand, you might be visible and influential within your company, a privileged position that may or may not be available to you on your own. My personal preference is to seek larger ponds once I am confident that I can handle the more powerful currents that are commonly found in such places.

The two most common ways to have a lot of money to invest are to start saving and investing early in life, and owning a successful business. Doing both is even better. You will seldom be paid as much for working for a company as you make owning a company that thrives. *Business Week* reported that the self-employed earn about 40 percent more hourly than those who work for others. This is one of the strong incentives for going into business for yourself. When a business for which you are well suited succeeds, it brings great joy to the heart.

Like mutual funds, starting a business covers the gamut in terms of degree of risk. Specific industries such as restaurants have high failure rates due largely to the percentage of people who jump in beyond their level of business expertise. It seems easy to many people who figure that if they can cook, they can also run a business. The perishable nature of the inventory adds further risk for restaurateurs. The more professional you are when you start a business, the more likely you are to succeed, however you measure success. Operating without a written plan, a business plan, is one of the most frequent shortcuts entrepreneurs take, and it is an error that ought to be remedied.

It is important to choose the right legal format for your business. The choices range from sole proprietorship to a partnership, to corporation. Each has advantages and disadvantages that vary with the size, complexity, and product or service the business provides. The most reliable rule of thumb is that C corporations are the best choice when your business becomes substantial in size. It is also the best format for a business that involves risk because individuals have more protection in a corporate environment than in a sole proprietorship or partnership.

One of the risks for sole proprietors and partners from a tax accounting point of view is the temptation to mingle business accounts with personal accounts. It is so easy to keep writing paychecks to yourself as you need them. Salaries are allowed only in a corporate structure. A sole proprietorship cannot pay the owner a salary, per se. Instead the owner takes a draw. It is important to keep draws on a regular and defined schedule. The best approach to paying yourself is to set your draw at your basic financial maintenance level and to pay yourself quarterly bonuses as the business permits after you determine how much of earnings is needed to help the business grow and how much needs to be set aside for taxes.

The tax structure favors making your other investments with your personal money rather than your company funds. Taxes are best paid with a business check. Bucket savings are just as appropriate for a business as they are for individuals. This is especially helpful when it comes time to make quarterly tax payments. Additional cash reserves may be accumulated for major purchases, be it a new computer or the building the business occupies. A savings account is one option for holding this money until it is needed. The interest earned on a company savings account is taxed on the proprietor's income on Schedule B so that it is not subject to self-employment tax.

I advise clients who are thinking of starting their own business to plan to start at a level proportionate to the base of security they already occupy. This does not mean to think small, but to choose a mountain to climb that is consistent with their equipment and experience. Start off part-time, if possible on evenings and weekends. The other advice I give is to be candid in their self-examination of their breadth of skills. Running a business requires far more than brilliance in a single aspect of the job.

There are many unhappy stories about starting or buying a small business. One unfortunate experience involves a man who wanted to retire from a particularly stressful job. He bought a business in Arizona at the peak of the market. His wife ran the business, which did not generate enough profits to service the debt. It failed after four years. It not only did not provide a jumping off point for his career change, it delayed his departure from the job he disliked because he needed to rebuild his retirement fund. Then he commuted to Arizona twice a month, and the stress of the travel and the absence from his wife added to their burdens. The business lost money, which provided a $1,000 per month savings in taxes. That was her only "income" for all her efforts. They deepened their problems by building a house in Arizona, and that mortgage became a burden.

It is also important to remain constructively skeptical. A business plan provides a blueprint for building the enterprise. It also unfailingly reveals gaps in the entrepreneur's knowledge of the business, the market, and competitive pressures and other obstacles that lurk beyond the walls of the office. While all businesses benefit from a business plan, they are essential for those businesses that move beyond the sole proprietor stage. Before you hire employees, invest in inventory, offices, equipment, and receivables, you need a business plan.

To build a business without a written plan is an invitation to drift off course. If you don't prune errant branches and tie the remaining ones into the shape you want to achieve, you get an eccentric and hard-to-manage business. Your business plan guides you, your partners, and your employees. A business plan provides an outline, and demonstrates that you understand your business and know where you are taking it.

Writing your business plan will bring financial issues clearly into focus. In order to generate the financial section of the plan you will clarify your cash resources, write a budget, make sales projections, anticipate tax obligations, and study your profit margins under a number of scenarios. This exercise greatly reduces the risk of unpleasant surprises as your business develops. It is time and effort well spent.

A business plan requires you to examine these questions in particular:

❑   What does your business do?

❑   What are the trends in that business?

❑ What makes your business unique or necessary?

❑ Who are your customers, and how will you reach them?

❑ What are your sales expectations and how will you handle sales and marketing?

❑ How many competitors do you have, who are they, and what are their advantages?

❑ How much will it cost to start your business and grow it?

❑ How many people does it take to execute your plan, and how will you organize them?

❑ What skills and experience do they need?

❑ What are the risks, and what will you do if they materialize?

The exercise of preparing a business plan forces you to examine fundamental issues such as your reasons for going into business in the first place and what your expectations of success really are.

Many businesses are begun without a written plan. Others that begin with a plan fail to update it so that it becomes irrelevant and therefore useless as a planning tool. An out-of-date business plan has little value as a reference point to determine the accuracy of earlier estimates and projections. Comparing projected costs and sales to the actual figures enables you to determine your degree of accuracy in making such projections. Being wrong is not a serious problem if you know how much and in which direction. Being wrong without any indication of whether you are high or low, left or right of your target, is an emergency situation because you can only guess at the best moves to make.

A thorough and up-to-date business plan serves many purposes:

❑ It provides a reference point for judging the accuracy of projections.

❑ It prevents lapses of memory from influencing decisions and evaluations based on historical data that have not been documented.

❑ It provides a written record of ideals, procedures, goals, and expectations that serve as a "constitution" for the purpose of holding to a steady course under pressure.

❑ It is a compelling document for persuading lenders and investors to act.

❑ Without a business plan, people are inclined to invent their own methods of handling a wide variety of situations. Once habits form it becomes nearly impossible to implement change. A business plan pays for itself many times over by serving as a blueprint and a statement of management philosophy. If you use the plan to obtain additional financing, it is even more valuable.

Most of the expenses for your own business, including hiring someone to assist you in writing a business plan, are fully deductible, and you pay 65 percent after taxes and Uncle Sam pays the rest. Wisdom dictates that you maintain separate bank accounts and charge cards for business and personal use to enable you to keep track of business expenses in a manner that will be clear to the IRS. Computers, once a source primarily of bafflement, have now reached the point of helpfulness to the business operator who is a computer novice. Money management programs like *Quicken*™ and *Quick Books*™ are easy to use and inexpensive, yet surprisingly versatile.

High risk activities

On the risk chart there is a line drawn between items 6 and 7 because I dislike the investments above the line. The last three investments, 7, 8 and 9, are too risky for me. These are, at best, investments for the discretionary part of your investment fund as distinct from the nest egg portion. Be prepared to lose all of your money if you choose any of these investments. If you can do that, and smile, you may want to put at least a small portion of your assets in these investments.

Investment number 7: speculative stocks

Speculative stocks may be a new issue with no track record, or a poor one. The company's liabilities may far exceed its assets. It is important to study both the downside risks and the potential that you think makes the risk worthwhile. Speculative stocks could double overnight or go to zero overnight.

Investment number 8: limited partnerships

Limited partnerships present a compound risk. You are exposed to both the partners and to the investment. In the 1970s and early 1980s limited partnerships became particularly popular as tax shelters, and the merits of the investment itself were often secondary. In a climate of outrageous income tax rates, limited partnerships have some appeal as taxpayers invest 19-cent dollars in these often speculative and high-overhead propositions. When the government is snagging 81 cents of each dollar, one tends to be more reckless with the remaining loose change if there seems to be an opportunity to double or triple what you have left by purchasing a limited partnership.

Tax shelters are always suspect. They became especially popular, or let me say, achieved notoriety, when income taxes exploded into the 80 percent bracket that President Reagan inherited when he came into office. The 1981 tax law, the Economic Recovery Tax Act (ERTA), reduced the maximum tax levels to 35 percent. This made tax shelters less appealing. The tax law of 1986 further reduced the value of tax shelters. The 1986 law was so complicated that it took two years of haggling in Congress to vote it through, and four more years for the lawmakers to explain how to interpret and apply the law. In the meantime taxpayers and tax advisors alike worked in a limbo where they had to make best-guesses in hope that their interpretations would not be too far from those that would emerge later from on high.

Limited partnerships typically charge 20 to 40 percent in start-up fees. Nowadays, tax shelters are obsolete, and limited partnerships that depend on tax sheltering as their claim to validity are equally obsolete.

When limited partnerships are created, money goes to the syndicator, and the broker may charge eight percent commission. An initial $10,000 partnership contribution shrinks to $8,000 or less to purchase the activity the limited partnership is supposed to be doing. We have seen windmills, oil and gas exploration, cable television, motion pictures, and aircraft leases. The popular one right now is low-income housing. Low-income housing partnerships have the advantage of tax credits, but you cannot write off losses, and limited partnerships are typically designed to have losses.

Losing such a large portion of your investment funds up front means that your $8,000 contribution has to earn 25% just to get back where you started. If it does, you still have an illiquid asset. Historically, real estate values don't support that investment, though they did briefly during the boom years in California's era of conspicuous consumption. While there have been spectacular stories of real estate values soaring in specific places during specific intervals, overall this has not been the trend. It has been calculated that if all the real estate in America had been sold in 1980 and again in 1994, the total proceeds would have been the same.

In trendy Orange County, California prices on office buildings have plunged. The *Orange County Business Journal* reported that "Some office properties are selling at discounts as deep as 60 percent off their late-1980s prices."[15] The story describes Colton Capital Corp.'s "feeding frenzy" as it acquired literally dozens of buildings at fire-sale prices. The dramatic discounts are at the expense of people who expected to put those inflated margins into their own pockets, not sacrifice them to rid themselves of poorly performing investments.

Prudential-Bache created an uproar in the 1980s selling risky limited partnerships. The Securities and Exchange Commission discovered what *Newsweek* magazine termed "an astonishing array of abuses: brokers had lied, traded customers' accounts excessively and persuaded customers to sign agreements they didn't understand. To settle the charges, Prudential agreed last fall to repay wronged investors."[17] Prudential lost $35,000,000 in the second quarter of 1994. Add to that the expense of paying back investors who got burned and the total rises to $215,000,000.

In California, Teachers Management & Investment Corporation (TMI) was sued to wrest control of the teachers' $1,000,000,000 (one-billion dollar) pension fund from the incumbent managers. The suit alleged the "largest and most devastating pension and retirement fraud in the history of California." The suit alleged that

TMI concealed $100,000,000 in debt and charged excessive fees of more than $4,000,000, and that the fund was insolvent. TMI's main strategy: <u>Real estate limited partnerships.</u> TMI blames the losses on the "substantially changed and depressed California real estate market."[17] Accountants Maurice Shuman and James Martin bought TMI in 1987. They set up a firm to develop partnership land and charged investors $1,000,000 a year, which they said was less than what other firms would charge. Some of the partnerships ended in bankruptcy, and others developed real estate that could not be sold.[18]

I have a client named Dorothy who lost $70,000 due to atrocious advice she received from a financial planner who persuaded her to invest $100,000 in limited partnerships. The advisor, a Certified Financial Planner, was recommended by Dorothy's boss. Dorothy describes herself as an artist, and uncomfortable with numbers. Dorothy says she was too shy to quiz the advisor on her qualifications, and felt that asking other clients about their experience would be "going behind her back." Dorothy now says that her advisor "Was a disaster for me. I trusted her. Another reason is that I wanted to support women."

When things started going badly, Dorothy says she wrote to her congressman, "Hey, I'm just a little old lady who is trying really hard to make some investments so I won't be a burden on society. You passed some income tax changes that really hurt me. It seems like every time they fiddle with the taxes, it's to my detriment. I just stick my money under the mattress now."

I bring considerable training in finance to bear on my personal decisions, and limited partnerships have not done well for me. During the early 1980s I invested in five of them under the umbrella of my individual retirement accounts. I invested $2,000 apiece in these partnerships after doing my homework as thoroughly as I knew how. None of these partnerships has come close to matching the wonderful projections that were presented to me. They haven't become worthless, but I could have done much better in less speculative investments. The good news is I made these inferior investments early in my career while I have time to make up for them. I no longer invest in limited partnerships.

Limited partnerships are illiquid investments. There is a poor secondary market for these partnerships. If you have to sell them before they mature, you are lucky to get 25 percent of your original investment back. Limited partnerships do not have a specified ending date. They are typically a seven-to-ten year investment, but there is no guarantee. I have seen limited partnerships which started in the 1970s which show no signs of maturing almost two decades later. Be especially wary of these and similar illiquid investments as you get older and have less time to recover from errors.

Investment number 9: oil & gas exploration

If you don't count the lottery or gambling in Las Vegas as investments, I nominate oil & gas exploration as the riskiest investment of all. This group also includes gold mine stock and deep-sea treasure hunting. Oil & gas exploration is very, very risky. There is no guarantee that your well is going to strike oil or gas even if you are drilling in a proven field. The odds are against you, and you must be prepared to lose your entire investment. You need to make certain that any potential gains are enough to offset the downside risks.

Riskier investments typically pay higher commissions to the person who makes the sale. It is important to understand the selling agent's motivations and to do business with one whose priority is to sustain a relationship with you, not to turn a quick profit at your expense. It is also important to balance your risk in a way that is appropriate both to you and your situation.

Chapter Six: Three Aspects of the Financial Transaction

There is only one good in the world—knowledge, and only one evil—ignorance.

—Aristotle

One of the great setbacks America suffered in the twentieth century was the virtual elimination of the front porch from the typical new home. The front porch encourages conversation of a particular sort. It is a conversation that you can drop in on without making any binding commitments of time. You can bring to it any level of folk wisdom, scholarship, anecdote, or fiction that you like. You can swap lies or quote Shakespeare. This form of communication promotes receptivity to a form of good luck known as serendipity. We find ourselves becoming increasingly lucky as we restore our vision of the world as a colorful and varied place to spend our lives.

Lacking a front porch myself, I endeavor to engage my clients over my desk. A generous amount of Lakers memorabilia and several jars brimming with candy relieve the atmosphere to some extent. It does not quite promote conversation like a front porch, but it works well enough. My appointments with clients typically last two hours. The paper work portion may fill half of this time or less. The rest of the time I use to learn my clients' priorities and values, and to hear about things that are on their financial horizons. I make it a point to address the whole person. I don't see how I can give good advice if I don't understand my clients and develop a genuine rapport with them. I bring to this counseling the proof that

I have the education to help them. My certificates on the wall testify to my preparation and study to do my job so we can settle down to solving their problems.

All financial transactions have three aspects:

- *Taxes*
- *Economics*

These are easy—they deal with numbers, and the accountant advises you on them.

- *Emotions*

This one is difficult, and is the client's job.

My job is to review the numbers with you, as often as necessary, until you have enough information to make a financial decision. Decision-making processes that omit one or two of the above considerations are likely to produce either poor decisions, or good decisions that don't hold up under pressure. The first two aspects are quantifiable, numerical, and relatively easy. The third is subjective, personal, and difficult.

Taxes

The tax implications of any investment can be defined by your accountant. That is what you pay your accountant to do. I recommend minimizing taxes in a prudent manner. Prudent, in this context, means that the effort to reduce taxes is secondary to the greater priority of increasing net worth. I say, with apologies to President John Kennedy, "Ask not how an expense can reduce taxes, ask how it can increase your net worth." I also caution that tax avoidance strategies can be so complex and time consuming that they hardly seem worth the effort when carried to extremes.

Prudent also means that you stay within the law. Another aspect of prudence is that you remain skeptical of tax gimmicks. Tax gimmicks are generally short-lived.

Tax laws change frequently. Annoyingly, they can change retroactively, thereby changing a seemingly good decision into a costly one. Tax reform in 1986 is a prime example of this. Many limited partnerships soured from a tax-shelter point of view because of retroactive changes in the tax code at that time. For this reason tax planning is, to some extent, a matter of making educated guesses. Decisions must be made with the expectation that the sands will shift to some extent. The more gimmicks a tax loophole includes, the more likely it is to be rescinded or altered at some point, unless it is an obscure loophole, in which case it may endure forever.

Rich and powerful people who influence tax laws are fond of devising laws that work to their benefit. They change those laws once the general population catches on to them and begins to copy their moves. The purpose of loopholes is to serve the elite, not the common citizen. Once they are too well known they are considered obsolete. If something in the tax code looks to you like a fad or a gimmick to benefit the rich, it probably is, and you are well off to assume that once it becomes popular its days are numbered. I prefer to stay with more stable, common-sense tax strategies.

Economics

Economics relates to the appropriateness of an investment to your budget and lifestyle. Investments ought to make sense. Can you afford a particular investment? Does it throw your overall financial picture out of balance, or does it complement it? The Picasso is magnificent, and perhaps a great investment, but do you have the $2 million? These two aspects of investing are the easy part. I can assist you with them. I can help you recognize when you have enough facts to make a sound decision.

One of the errors I see most frequently is the human tendency to second guess decisions that were thoughtfully made. A decision based on knowledge and diligence is best respected. Even if things turn out differently from what you expected, the merits of your decision ought not to be questioned because this tends to erode confidence the next time you are faced with a decision. It is important to recognize that you are not responsible for the elements you cannot control. A reasonable assessment of probabilities is all you can accomplish. The final outcome is beyond all of our powers to predict.

I encourage clients to answer these questions about the probable outcome of an investment decision: What is the best thing that can happen? What is the worst thing that can happen? What is the most likely thing to happen? It helps to assign numbers to each segment of the question. Consider this quantitative analysis summarizing the potential of a $1,000 investment.

Quantitative Analysis				
Scenario	Outcome	$ Value of Asset in 5 years	Probability (must total 100%)	Quantitative Analysis
Best	Big increasse in value	2000	25	500
Worst	Decrease in value	700	25	175
Most likely	Moderate increase in value	1200	50	600
			Most likely result of investment:	$ 1275

This table can include more outcomes. It depends on the usefulness and validity of each separate option as to how many you include. It is not worthwhile to make calculations that are purely speculative. Also, it is important that the percentages total 100. Multiply the percentage of probability times the projected asset value, and put this number in the right-hand column. Add the right-hand column for a final tally of what the asset is most likely to be worth in five years.

Reducing a lot of facts and estimates to a table like this makes it much easier to grasp visually what might otherwise be a jumble of 'ifs, ands, or buts,' and it makes it possible for a group of people to be sure they are synchronized with one another in their understanding of the subject that is being discussed. A resistance to this type of analysis of an investment beforehand is a flag that marks hidden emotional currents. It is a symptom of the attitude,

"My mind is made up, don't confuse me with the facts."

You can use this simple exercise as a litmus test to determine how detailed your understanding of the business aspects of the proposition is. Challenge the numbers you provide, or invite other people to challenge them, and respond with compelling arguments based on facts to support your estimates. If the numbers are assigned based on pure hope, that will quickly become evident under scrutiny. If emotion is inflating your expectations of the investment, this exercise will reveal that fact. Then you can decide if the potential gain is worth the risk.

Here is an empty template that you can use for your calculations.

Quantitative Analysis				
Scenario	Outcome	$ Value of Asset in 5 years	Probability (must total 100%)	Quantitative Analysis
Best	Big increasse in value			
Worst	Decrease in value			
Most likely	Moderate increase in value			
Most likely result of investment: $				

Need for an investment specialist

In the best of worlds, a specialist would merely be beneficial to your financial life. In a business climate where your government makes a concerted effort to baffle you so that you will make mistakes and have to pay penalties and interest, a specialist is indispensable. Complexity creates a private club. Once the masses learned to read, the elite needed a new advantage. They invented the tax code.

Lloyd Bentsen's 1987 long form tax return saved him $146,282 compared to what he would have paid using the short form 1040. The government makes out big if you opt for simplicity.[19]

The *1994 United States Master Tax Guide*, published and updated yearly by Commerce Clearing House, runs 660 pages of fine print. The *1994 Guidebook To California Taxes*, explains California tax law (in 635 pages of slightly larger print). Specialists form close relationships with these dreary texts. You don't want to do that. Instead, you pay a specialist to get you through tax planning as quickly and as painlessly as possible. When the government speaks of paperwork reduction, they don't mean yours.

The IRS, wanting to close a breach in the tax system, mandated that restaurant owners would have to participate in extracting taxes on tips paid to servers. It was such an oppressive and burdensome way to approach the problem that 69 legislators formally protested. Further, the IRS threatened to audit businesses that did not comply with their demands. The audits were punitive. The coercive powers of the government are substantial. Bullying is both mean-spirited and lazy. Such tactics ought to bring a storm of protest upon the head of anyone who uses them.

It is unfortunate that our country is highly adversarial. It is even more unfortunate that the government is often an adversary. You need a financial advisor who is not merely competent, but will befriend you. This word means to favor, countenance, and give aid, and you need those things when dealing with the government. At best, you will find an advisor who understands your whole value system as it relates to money and money management. This advisor will help you define the advantages and disadvantages of each investment you are considering in the context of your needs and value system.

You also need someone with whom you comfortably can share the intimate details of your financial affairs. One of the reasons people are reluctant to change accountants is that they do not want to experience a painful transition during which they risk annoyance or embarrassment, or both. Make the effort early in your career to find financial advisors you trust and like, and then stay with them.

Emotions

The third aspect of a financial transaction, the emotional one, is much more difficult to manage, and authority over it can <u>never</u> be transferred to another person. I know many people whose strong emotions influence their seemingly rational decisions, but they do not recognize these emotions on a conscious level. These undercurrents are the most troublesome part of finance for many people. Some people think it odd that I have studied both accounting and psychology, and perhaps it is, but it has provided me with insights into the struggles people experience with the emotional aspects of money.

The language we use to describe money transactions indicates our desire for safety and predictability. We create a *trust* to enable us to preserve and pass on our property. A company issues a *bond* to join the investor with the company. An investment *matures*, meaning it grows for a proper period of time appropriate to itself. A property can *appreciate* in value. On the other hand, a check not backed by money is *dishonored*.

The word broke is revealing. Being without money denotes a break in the circulation of wealth. Money, the paper and metal symbols of wealth, we call *currency*. We call it that because it is something that flows in a current. Break the current, and we are separated from the community, and we lack money.

Our coins display the motto, "IN GOD WE TRUST." We collectively seek assurances that we are being watched over and blessed in the area of money. The appeal to deity would not likely get past the American Civil Liberties Union in these times, but our founding fathers deemed it appropriate, and probably necessary. As a nation, we want to put our emotions in a peaceful state, and we strive for this on an individual level too, each in our own way.

Darlene, a successful office machine sales person, was isolated from money until she left home. Her lack of experience with responsibility for money left her unprepared for handling money in adulthood. She tells her story:

> The first experience I had of freedom of choice
> with money was when I left home. Prior to that I

100

had certain jobs, and my mother insisted all my income go in the bank and I live on $1 a week. I never knew how much money was in the account. Then in 1972 I discovered that I had $1,700 in the bank, I had delusions of grandeur. I made some terrible choices in spending money because the dollar a week thing hadn't worked. I didn't know what values were important, or how to spend money. That was the first experience I had with money.

The second momentous experience I had was when they repossessed my car. I hadn't made any payments, and I didn't think it was a big deal. It was the day that I was supposed to drive from Chicago to Dallas to have a job change. A girl friend had flown in from Washington DC to make the drive with me. We had packed the car the night before, and it had everything that I didn't put on the truck.

My friend Ann said, "Haven't you made payments?" I said, Yeah, but not really. She was angry, I think, and she ended up flying back. I had to fly to Dallas. I think that was the bottom of my barrel. I am totally lost without my car, and it was the first car I had bought brand-new. It was a very tough lesson to learn.

I realized then there are organizations out there I am responsible to. I don't think I had learned a lot after spending the $1,700 over that 9-12 month period. I made all those decisions, and they were wrong. I had no idea that the $1,700 would be gone so fast. That was in my twenties, and ten years later I still had no idea. There was an adult part of me that knew there was an organization out there called GMAC that could repossess my car. But it wasn't going to happen to me. Naiveness went into it. Both incidents have that in common. I was very naive. I was very unwilling to accept the seriousness and the repercussions of my decision.

I don't want to be obligated to anyone. I don't want to have anybody holding anything over my head saying...I don't want to have my car taken away again. There is always this overshadowing fear that somebody's going to suffocate me, that somebody's going to tell me what to do.

Darlene now shares responsibility for raising two teenage girls from her husband's previous marriage. She says she and her husband are "extremely, extremely open with them and give them every opportunity to express their freedom of choice."

The girls' mother, according to Darlene, is extremely frugal. The daughters quarrel over how frequently they can buy hair conditioner. Sometimes they ask Darlene to buy it for them. Angela tells her mother that buying hair conditioner is a mother's responsibility. Darlene says that her focus is on teaching the girls to recognize the choices they have, and to identify the repercussions that follow each one. Then, she says, she emphasizes giving them the freedom of choice and avoids judging them for the choices they make.

Darlene says that the contrast between her values about money and the girls' mother's values confused the girls at first. Now that the older girl is 17 she is choosing her own values. She is quick to back her mother into corners with logic, and her mother's only recourse is to demand cooperation on the basis of the mother-daughter relationship. Darlene says that their mother's fall back device to influence her daughters is the demand, "Because I say so."

Darlene does not discuss money with her own mother. She says, "There is too much in me that is like my own mother." She is not close to her mother, who came from Yugoslavia with visions of grandeur about the possibilities in America in the years immediately following World War II. Her father had already been here for seven years, working as a cab driver and saving money.

Darlene says she and her mother both derive a great deal of security from material possessions. Darlene chose sales because she believed that sales people have no restraints or limits on their earning potential. She says she has a keen interest in lifestyle issues and works to achieve in order to compete with, or impress her mother. She buys what she wants and worries about paying for it later. Darlene does not balance her checkbook, but she does balance her husband's. His frugal style with money is antithetical to hers, but she says they never argue about money or how to spend it.

Disturbed emotions

While I don't have any severely disturbed clients, there are plenty of them in this world. We need to acknowledge that severe emotional problems are often at the base of money issues. In such instances no amount of classroom lecture on prudence will make much difference. If a person believes at a deep level that he is unworthy of success as he defines it, he will find a way to ignore or defeat any advice. We are all emotionally disturbed to some degree. It may be a small degree, or it may be nearly overwhelming. Far reaching studies of this subject are available, and the bibliography provides some additional resources for the reader who wants to pursue it.

Let's acknowledge that our society is massively addicted. An addiction is an activity that harms us, and we know it, but we keep doing it anyway. Addiction is usually a matter of degree. The most dangerous substances, like heroin, are so powerful that to use them nearly equates with becoming addicted. Less powerful addictions are more common. They include addictions to drugs (including alcohol and tobacco), sex, violence, perfectionism, religion, eating disorders, and money. An addiction is a compulsive relationship to any mood altering activity that has life damaging consequences. We turn to addictions, primarily, because we think that we are in some way inferior in a manner that is beyond repair, and the addictive activity seems to be what we "deserve."

How did we come to be so addicted in this country? According to author and therapist John Bradshaw, we become addicted because we learned, one way or another, to distrust our own emotions and instincts. Our guidance system is ignored, or it sends us signals that we mistrust. We then gravitate to addictions because they provide intense experiences, they are readily available, and they produce a lifestyle that seems to match what we think we deserve.

If you are addicted in a way that affects money in your life, you will need to get to the roots of the addiction before theories and techniques will have any real meaning for you.

Money madness

What does "rich" mean? Who is rich? Webster's dictionary begs the question by saying that "rich" means having wealth, or having "much money." It doesn't say how much. President Clinton continues to redefine the word rich. During his campaign he promised to increase taxes only on the rich. Then he signed a tax increase that affects people making $20,000 per year or more. Only the president considers $20,000 evidence of being rich.

There is a widespread tendency to spend more than we make, arguably on the premise that we don't have much money, but if we did we would be happier. Much of this is the simple result of thinking that our personal experience expands as our money supply expands. Rich is a subjective term and one that yields meaning to each individual only upon reflection and the application of imagination. The definition of rich isn't a problem so much as it is a mystery. It is a subject to contemplate in a leisurely way. For purposes of discussion, let us say that rich people are those for whom substantial burdens such as home mortgages, tuition to private colleges for the kids, and regular and frequent services of professionals to advise them, are no problem from a money-supply point of view. Having these things does not equate with happiness, but it can qualify us as rich.

The "disease of me"

Some people pursue money with much the same mind set as body builders pursue muscle. They are working to sculpt themselves into an exaggerated figure that will ultimately be judged by other people. They are working primarily for something to display. The parallel goes further. I see a similarity between the overheated desire for wealth for its own sake with the use of steroids by body builders and other athletes. Steroids and other chemicals dull our awareness of elemental sensations and focus our attention only on the extremes, the performance peaks.

I recommend that you learn to enjoy all your money. Enjoy each dollar, not just the sight of stacks of them. Choose the highest use of each dollar. You can only spend them once!

O. J. Simpson seemed to have it all. His palatial home, prestige, and wealth were impressive. His finances were rocked by his devastating experience of being accused of the murders of his former wife, Nicole Brown Simpson, and her friend, Ronald Goldman. Having it all runs deeper than having power, wealth, and fame. Having it all rests on a base of internal serenity.

Sports and entertainer salaries have gone crazy, perhaps as players searched for financial fulfillment. Ryne Sandberg signed a contract in 1992 to play second base for the Chicago Cubs in exchange for $28,400,000. The Mets agreed to pay Bobby Bonilla $5,800,000. Bill Cosby made $58,000,000 in 1991. Oprah Winfrey made $42,000,000 that same year. Provided that these people invest their money well, their income snowballs. It is difficult for most of us to imagine such wealth being available to us.

Because their wealth often comes suddenly, the show-business rich are often susceptible to terrible advice from people whose credentials suggest they should know better. Many advisors encourage their clients to make investments that reduce taxes but which don't address the real issue: increasing net worth. Short, high-trajectory careers bring unique retirement planning needs compared to the average person. Most of us have a career lasting thirty to fifty years during which we build up an investment portfolio to provide a retirement income Celebrities often face a short timeline, and many just get a taste of fame and wealth.

Fame must be supported by a strong ego. Actor Tony Curtis once told an interviewer that he has two careers: acting and fame. He noted that being good at one did not guarantee success with the other. Strong egos are essential, yet they can make people impervious to advice and counsel. Ego is out of hand when it produces feelings of invincibility. Ego needs to be tempered with common sense.

In his autobiography, Magic Johnson comments:[20]

> When you're playing, it's so easy to get caught up in the glamour. Everybody tells you how great you are, and you start to believe you can walk on water. You think the future will take care of itself. But unless you make real plans, you're going to end up in trouble.

To underscore the extremes ego can reach, consider the assassination of André Escobar who played on the Columbian soccer team. According to a *Los Angeles Times* article, a spectator killed him because he inadvertently kicked the ball into his own team's goal during the World Cup 1994. That was a capital offense in the deranged mind of the killer. The game was that important to him.

Pat Riley notices inflamed egos. Mark Heisler wrote about it in the *Los Angeles Times*. Riley refers to the condition as the "disease of me." Too much awareness of the self that destroys team spirit and leads players to question any decision by the coach that does not flatter their ego. He was quoted asking, "Why has it gotten that way in the NBA that players say, 'He didn't talk to me?' These guys are pros, making millions of dollars. Their job is to come and play, accept a role."

Riley's comments get stronger: he notes the "self-centered, greed-oriented, defiant attitudes" running rampant in the NBA, which he believes, "are going to bring this league down." Riley did not renew his contract with the Knicks. Would you hesitate to sign a contract that would pay you $3,000,000 per year, $8,219 per day? It takes something pretty serious to make someone hesitate in the face of that offer. This same pressure caused Billy Cunningham to retire from coaching the Philadelphia Seventy-Sixers while he was at the top of his career.

High-flying careers often hit air pockets. A critic lamented of

Eddie Murphy, "The onetime box-office ruler practically begged viewers to see *Beverly Hills Cop III*." Len Bias, after being drafted by the Boston Celtics, overdosed on drugs the same night. We are all writing in the sands of time. Our marks are short-lived.

Advice that superstars rarely hear

The usual advice from professionals is to buy a house with a big mortgage as a write-off, and it is unsound, particularly for a person who may not have a career in five years. Magic Johnson reports that his accountant advised him "not to make too large a down payment." He put down $6.2 million anyway, and "a few months later, I wrote out a check for that last million." Magic says he does not like debt.

This is my advice for superstars. Take as an example someone who makes a salary of $1,000,000 per year. After taxes the star has $650,000 in cash. The bad advice would be to put 20 percent down ($500,000) on a house worth $2,500,000. I recommend paying in cash for a $500,000 house. This leaves a balance of $150,000. Next, invest this $150,000 in an account paying 4 percent (a figure that is conservative to the point of gloominess). This investment generates $6,000 a year to pay property taxes and insurance on the paid-for $500,000 home. This means that if you do not make another dime in Hollywood or in the sporting arena, you still have a generously comfortable home for the rest of your life.

Singer Ron Holman achieved a single success with a song called *Love You So*. He toured with oldies-but-goodies shows but never recorded another hit song. He amused his audiences with the line, "I would now like to sing a medley of my hit." If your career resembles Holman's, this advice is for you. In that case even a modest income will be enough to live on since you face no mortgage and have provided for property taxes and insurance on your home.

Ego vs common sense

Bumper stickers are a bizarre, but often informative, index of what is going on in our collective consciousness. Consider this message: "The difference between men and boys is the cost of their toys." Or this one, popular in 1987: "The one who dies with the most toys wins." As you get richer, you are more inclined to buy toys such as boats (not the bath tub variety!), vacation cabins, or fancy cars. You might even fall prey to what I consider one of the all-time bad investments, condominium time shares. In any event, my advice is to rent the object of your desire a few times before you commit to a purchase. This is the equivalent of dating for a good period of time before you marry. Much of our attraction to toys is more lust than love. In those instances, it is cheaper in the long run to pay a premium for the short term and rent the object.

In Kareem Abdul-Jabbar's first autobiography, he recounts the story of Wilt Chamberlain's influence on his youthful transition into the world of wealth and power. "Anything you could think of that a seventeen-year-old wants, Wilt had," he wrote. "We drove up in his Bentley to see his horse run. Wilt owned a trotter."[21] Kareem wrote that he had never before seen anybody "piss-away money." Do you need a Bentley? Do you need a trotter? Only you can answer these questions, but I can advise you about the process you use to decide. The process involves having the experience, or a version of it, at minimal expense to determine if it is genuine for you before you commit to it. A handy bit of advice is to know how you can get out of something—and how much getting out will cost—before you get into it.

My advice to the super rich, should any of them read these pages, is to heed Magic's advice. If you will pardon the pun, keep your feet on the ground.

Chapter Seven: Win-win and Character Values

Thou shalt love thy neighbor as thyself.
—**Mark 12:31**

W in-win is a wonderful concept that Stephen Covey explains in detail in *The 7 Habits of Highly Effective People*. Covey explains that many years ago our country shifted its emphasis from character strength as a key to success and began to concentrate instead on techniques and gimmicks. He calls for a return to basic values. So do I.

Our American tradition is one in which a winner implies a loser. This is especially obvious in sports where ranking first is almost the only goal that gains respect. In California's premium wine industry a bronze medal is considered by many to be a handicap, and is all but kept secret by those who are tainted by owning one. Only a gold medal matters.

I am deeply concerned that we have formalized, and seem committed to intensifying, our collective efforts to punish rather than to mentor people. The United States prison population topped 1,000,000 in 1994. This number is deceptively low because another half million are in jail, a distinction that merely indicates a shorter stay. Experts predict it will get worse quickly.

The school system is crumbling due to lack of money to maintain the infrastructure, and endless controversy over issues ranging from bilingual teaching to what books can be in the school libraries add more stress. We shorten public library hours and open more prisons. The response to conflict is all too often to create a stalemate. The lose/lose mentality is highly visible and sets an example for our children from their earliest years.

This mentality of self-righteousness and machismo, which is supported by generations of tradition, inevitably pervades our government. Politicians went to school. They were trained by the same system that we see in our neighborhoods. Combine righteousness with bureaucracy, and you have a formidable obstacle to change. The government, historically, has remained ignorant of new business developments and has seen its role primarily as an agent of discipline, a scolding parent vigilant over reckless business people. Its job has been to restrain and interfere with private enterprise after it has caused trouble. It reacts after problems become large.

This posture is in stark contrast to Japan where government is seen as a body whose job it is to nurture young industries and to promote meso-economics, the dynamics of certain industries and sectors. Japan, incidentally, has the lowest incarceration rate in the world. We would do well to ask why.

During the industrial revolution a mold was created for an image of the successful business man. It included a large amount of greed and an eagerness to act to the detriment of society at large if it produced huge wealth for the business. Such people were the epitome of smugness and complacency once they achieved success and market domination. More recently, Eastman Kodak, General Motors, IBM, and the U. S. Postal service serve as examples of American management arrogance and complacency. A win-win mentality would have prevented the hardening-of-the-attitudes that proved so costly to all of these organizations.

Kodak has mounted a half-dozen management overhauls in the last decade. They have reduced the work force from 145,300 in 1988 to well under six figures. They are notorious for their inability to lower costs. They created $10,000,000,000 in debt by entering the health care field. Management errors cost employees their jobs.

These are expensive mistakes. Mistakes like these have a ripple effect throughout our society.

Adversarial bureaucracy is not limited to government and business. Consider our institutions of higher learning. Thomas Toch reported in *U.S. News & World Report* that at Harvard University, founded in 1636, there are 10 largely autonomous faculties. Provost Jerry Green resigned after 21 months on the job, reportedly out of frustration at resistance to his efforts to merge them. At Columbia and Yale, faculty members protested mightily when attempts were made to eliminate less productive departments.

Harvard's president, Neil Rudenstine, was ordered by his doctor to take an indefinite leave due to stress. He needed to raise, $1,000,000 per day to reach fund-raising goals. The cost to operate Harvard is $68,400 per student per year. Harvard has a prestigious business school that, we must assume, strives to teach its students to manage change in large organizations, yet I wonder if they are doing this work in their own institution.

Big money power struggles

General Motors is said to have the worst supplier relationships in Detroit. Suppliers are angry. GM does things like showing suppliers' drawings to their competitors, grinding them relentlessly on price, and emphasizing price over responsiveness and quality. GM likes to get deep price concessions, then offer the job to a Chinese company or other offshore manufacturer for even greater bargaining leverage. GM was desperate after losing $4,500,000,000 in 1992 and even more than that in 1991. It squeezed part of its losses out of suppliers. The company is actively destroying its relationships with suppliers and is committed to a win-lose management style.[23]

How are things in China where GM gets competitive quotes? Foreign-funded factories employ about 6,000,000 Chinese, many of whom are children. In the summer of 1994 a minimum working age of 16 was established, along with a maximum six-day work week as a move against labor abuses. It is not the Chinese who create all the problems. Joint ventures are among the worst offenders in terms of human rights.[23] Working conditions are at least as bad as they were during the nadir of the industrial revolution in our nation. Official reports from China listed 45,000 industrial accidents in Guangdong in 1993 resulting in 8,700 deaths. Workers are beaten, strip-searched, and given dangerous and obsolete equipment to operate. The trade union is government controlled. These are the same folks that sponsored the Tiananmen Square massacre. With unemployment and inflation out of control, and the government arresting those who protest working conditions, the rank and file worker doesn't have many cards to play. Corporate bullies can have a field day using Chinese price quotes for leverage against American manufacturers.

People tend to live up to, or down to, expectations. We set expectations, and we announce what those expectations are by our actions. In the summer of 1994 the professional baseball industry began its eighth strike in 23 years. Walter Shapiro wrote in *Time* magazine, "Never before has the naked power struggle between players and owners seemed so heedless and self-destructive."[24]

The owners of the baseball franchises have privileged status in that they have a special exclusion from antitrust laws. They don't have to play by the same rules as other businesses. Do they use this privilege with the fans in mind? Do they care about the long-term viability of the sport? The fans ultimately pay the bill.

If we are witnessing the corruption of the spirit of fair play in our national sport for all to see, how will we persuade corporate leaders making deals in China to be decent and considerate of anonymous workers in those faraway countries?

It seems clear to me that the attitudes we model for children stay with them. They grow up to run businesses with the attitudes they were taught by our example. We have to break the cycle by changing the way we operate locally.

Individuality is the key to win-win thinking

It is common to use the accumulation of money as an index of success. When money becomes a competition with other people, the exercise is painful. *Desiderata* reminds us, "If you compare yourself with others, you may become vain and bitter; for always there will be greater and lesser persons than yourself. Enjoy your achievements and plans. Keep interested in your career."

The reason comparisons don't work is that each of us is <u>unique</u>. We are inevitably comparing apples and oranges, as the saying goes. It is not currently in fashion to celebrate individuality, so arguments in favor of idiosyncrasies tend to be ignored or sound contrived. A forced comparison by some arbitrary measure is necessarily frustrating. Even in a narrow area of specialization there are differences. Equally talented tennis players will find themselves less evenly matched when they switch playing surfaces, say from hardcourt to grass, or when they play doubles instead of singles. Close examination reveals differences. Simplistic comparisons are tiring and largely futile. Win-win cultivates an appreciation of differences, and these differences reveal that we each want highly individualistic goals that can readily coexist.

Win-win requires us to find combinations that work. This applies as much to combinations within the range of our personal choices as it does in the corporate world and on the level of national and global politics.

Win-win in daily life

How does win-win work in everyday life? It starts in small ways. Here is an example, and it is not appropriate for many people, but I want to mention it because it is typical of the kind of thinking that goes with win-win. When a home owner sells a house, the bank usually gets involved. It charges a lot of money for this service. It is an advantage to both seller and buyer if the bank can be kept out of the transaction. If the seller carries all or part of the paper, he or she can charge an interest rate lower than the bank charges and still make more money than the bank offers depositors. The buyer saves relative to obtaining the same amount of money from a bank.

This arrangement can be modified to a format known as 30-due-in-5. This means that the monthly payments are structured as though the loan would extend for 30 years, but after five years a balloon payment is required to retire the loan. This requires the buyer to refinance the loan. This can produce as much as a five percent gain for both parties during the life of the loan compared to working through a bank.

The Golden Rule, treat others the way you want to be treated, is the most reliable guide to human relations I have ever found. I have a client who speaks of the Platinum Rule, which he defines as "Treat yourself the way you treat other people." He says it is especially useful for people who don't treat themselves as well as they treat other people, and, more broadly, it makes the doer more aware of the impact of his actions on others. Both rules work in a way that successfully crosses cultural and political boundaries. I have clients who came to this country from Argentina, Jamaica, Pakistan, Viet Nam, Ireland, and 16 other countries. I have clients in more than 20 states with whom I communicate by phone, fax, postal service, and e-mail because our relationship works so well they are willing to tolerate the inconvenience that distance imposes.

Ninety-five percent of my clients came to me through referrals by other clients who like the way I handle their accounts. I take telephone calls during appointments. This is part of my commitment to being available. I don't hide from my clients, and when I take a call, I assure the client I'm with that the time goes on the caller's bill, not the client who is present. Following the Golden Rule produces a lifestyle for me that I like, and it seems to please a lot of other people as well. The Golden Rule leaves a positive imprint. It is imperative that our government be run by people who put the Golden Rule at the core of their value system.

I recommend a thorough and patient reading of Stephen Covey's *The 7 Habits of Highly Effective People*. Covey advocates forming only those bargains that serve all the participants. Win-win or no deal, is his recommendation. Win-win can only work on a foundation of respect for life. Win-win is a way of life that suits people who have a vision and a high degree of self-confidence. It is nearly impossible to convince small-minded or mean-spirited people to adopt it. It is only after repeated experiences in win-lose encounters that they tire of them and look for other possibilities.

Serendipity is that fortunate coincidence that brings some advantage they were not seeking. Serendipity, I suspect, happens more often to those who seek to make their presence beneficial to others.

Cheating on taxes

According to a *Time* magazine article published in 1983, in the early days of the income tax citizens considered cheating on taxes to be on a par with stealing from the poor box at church. Whether this is true or not, I don't know. I do know that a lot of people have an adversarial relationship with taxes today. The unofficial methods of avoiding taxes are many: Work for cash (which includes most criminal transactions and countless common place legitimate services), don't file a return, file but don't bother to pay, pad expenses, barter off-the-record instead of selling for cash, don't report capital gains, and make transactions so elaborate and convoluted that nobody wants to examine them for taxes due.

The Treasury Department says that the number of bogus electronic tax refunds in 1993 reached 58,828 and cost an amount some estimate to be $5,000,000,000. With more than 13,500,000 returns coming in over the wire, this is a small number in terms of percentage, but it is expensive in terms of dollars lost.

This is a good time to clarify three terms that relate to taxes: tax avoidance, tax deferral, and tax evasion. Tax avoidance is a legal maneuver, such as tax-free municipal bonds, that makes money immune to taxation. You don't owe the government taxes for whatever reason. Tax deferral means that you get to legally postpone the payment of taxes, but you do owe them, they are on the books. IRAs are an example of an investment in which the earnings are not taxed until a later time. Tax evasion means that you owe taxes but you don't pay them. This is a criminal act. I see no cleverness in tax evasion. Proper tax planning provides ample tax avoidance. If that is not enough for you, lobby Congress for new laws.

Lots of famous people get in trouble for taxes. Vice President

Spiro Agnew pleaded no contest in 1973 to charges of evading $13,551 in taxes due on money received from influence-seekers while Governor of Maryland. Jimmy Carter's brother Billy lost his home and service station to the IRS who sold them to raise money. Al Capone got hung up on a tax charge while his real nastiness and violence toward people went unpunished. There are plenty of more recent stories, too.

The IRS printed a poster with Capone's picture on it and the caption, "You can get away with murder until you cheat on your taxes."

What are the chances of getting caught? Overall, audit rates on individuals fell from 1.06 percent in 1992 to .92 percent in 1993. Corporations saw a slight increase in audits from 3.04 percent in 1992 to 3.05 percent the following year. There are many more corporate than individual audits, but audits of corporations yield more than twice as much in taxes as audits on individuals. Large estate settlements have audit rates of 30 to 50 percent. Statistically the likelihood of getting caught through an audit increases with your income. Returns showing taxable income of $50,000 or more, and there are some three or four million of them each year, are audited at a rate of about one in twenty. The largest group of returns is for incomes under $10,000 per year, about 35,000,000 of them. They have about one chance in two hundred of an audit.

There is also a higher incidence of audits in the western states. The rate there is 1.34 percent. The mid-Atlantic states have the lowest rate, just over .5 percent. Now, getting caught doesn't always mean you have to pay. The IRS admits that it is owed billions that it can't lay its hands on. In many cases they are willing to bargain.

Apart from what other people do, and apart from what you can do if you have nerves of steel, what is the path of action and the mental posture that results in peace of mind?

I recommend playing the tax game skillfully and as much by the spirit of the law as the law itself will permit. The result will be that you abide by the rules and hand over an amount of money to the government that is determined as much as possible by your wit and planning. You can be proud of your performance in playing well and also of your dedication to keeping agreements. If you are not satisfied with your tax burden after playing by the rules it is time to change the rules.

It is tempting to take shortcuts rather than do the hard work of creating change. Over time, shortcuts lead to the collapse of ethical systems. Tax evasion provides a short term gain with a tremendous long term penalty. For village elders particularly, it is imperative to abide by the law, and to demonstrate a commitment to changing laws that are out of date or inappropriate in other ways. Short cuts and dodges are corrosive to the system they work to defeat.

Finances are part of the ecology of our social life. Any approach that is less comprehensive, any approach that attempts to isolate money from the rest of our values in order to "make it behave," is doomed to fail.

Five times as many Americans as Japanese think that "the only real goal of a company is making a profit."[25] Americans feel this more strongly than any of the twelve nationalities surveyed by the authors of *The Seven Cultures of Capitalism*. The survey revealed that Americans are also the most extreme in their view that a company is a set of tasks, not an organization of people, a view that is the polar opposite of the Japanese view. It is time for citizens of the United States to recognize that the country has recreated itself through immigration. We have to reunite the United States with a vision that crosses cultural boundaries.

We no longer work beside our parents at their craft. Fewer and fewer of us work a lifetime for a single employer. Fortunately there are many pioneering efforts to reinvent work. Increasingly we are discovering that our unique combination of skills, interests and experiences distinguishes us from our peers. This opens the door to working joyfully. At the heart of this development of uniqueness is a desire to return each individual to his or her labor of love. This involves joining work and income as inseparable values so that we do the work we love and accept the money that flows from that activity. When we find the right work we tend to find the right income level as well. When we see work as an expression of our deepest longing, the temptation to use our position in the work place to wrench money from the system tends to fall away.

We find adversarial relationships in high places such as the world of professional baseball. We find them in low places where gangs fight their wars in our city streets. The solution to both is win-win thinking. The <u>best</u> news is that win-win is not just a pleasant ideal. The world needs to hear this about win-win:

- ❑ **It produces results that <u>can be measured</u>.**
- ❑ **It is <u>teachable</u>**
- ❑ **It simply <u>works better</u> than win-lose.**

It has been scientifically proven that being "nice" works. If you want to read a scholarly treatment about this, I recommend *The Evolution of Cooperation* by Robert Axelrod.

Win-win is an idea for the real world. Being nice is <u>more profitable</u> than any other strategy.

Section II
Money and relationships

Chapter Eight: Money and Your Mate

The first male illusion about women is that daily stress shouldn't diminish her sexuality any more than it does yours.

—Johnathan Kramer and Diane Dunaway

M en and women are different. It is a fascinating study, and I encourage everyone to pursue it. I learned, for example, that stress over money affects women differently than it does men. Excellent books on the subject are listed in the bibliography; the quotation above comes from *Why Men Don't Get Enough Sex and Women Don't Get Enough Love.* In this world we have the relationship problems that are built into us by nature plus the constraints manufactured by the people who make tax laws. Between the two, money in relationships is a thorny issue. Give yourself all the advantages you can.

If tax law is any indication, the IRS does not like marriage and wants to discourage it. There are several marriage penalties in the tax code, and I mention some of them in this book. The level of absurdity of these penalties is characteristic of the IRS. Consider that someone who travels for business reasons can deduct a prescribed amount of money for meals taken on trips unless that taxpayer is related to his or her employer. Marriage is complicated enough without the financial pressures our government puts on it.

The government has acted improperly by establishing tax code that discourages marriage by taxing it. Would we be tolerant of a relative who offered money on the condition that we remained unmarried? Senators and representatives are so bold as to take this position with the nation. For whom do they speak?

Consider that two wage earners who live together pay less in taxes before they marry than afterward. The government provides an incentive for cohabitation rather than for marriage. The brouhaha over family values during the Bush-Quail campaign against Clinton-Gore was mostly empty posturing and chest beating. The tax code is where the rubber meets the road in politics, and the tax code is definitely anti-family.

If you are a POSSLQ (say pozzlecue), a Person of Opposite Sex Sharing Living Quarters, this facet of the tax code is likely to cost you around $1,000 per year should you decide to exercise your right to marry your favorite POSSLQ.

Bill and Nancy got a divorce and kept it secret from their friends and family in spite of continuing to live together. They told me they did it for tax purposes. Later they did announce their divorce and separate from one another, but it was several years after the fact.

It is important to be aware of what the government considers sham transactions. They weigh what they call "facts and circumstances." They look at things that fall into the gray area. An example is a divorce by a couple who are past 55 years of age so that they can get separate onetime exclusions on the capital gain on the sale of their home. The government offers double the exemption to divorced people compared to married owners of real estate. The $125,000 exclusion produces a tax savings of about $40,000. Is it worth getting a divorce to save that amount of money? I think it is hideous that government prompts us to think about it. This amount of money means different things to different people.

For those of us willing to defy the tax man and marry anyway, we find obstacles and rewards ahead of us. Therapist and counselor Harville Hendrix teaches that we can only discover the best about ourselves when we are in committed relationships. The pressures of responsibility, and the improvement that results from caring feedback create a situation that refines us, like ore that is turned to fine steel by heat and pressure. All wholesome relationships improve us, and marriage is the strongest influence because it is the most intense, personal, and lasting relationship of our life.

One of the ironies of marriage, psychologists say, is that we often marry a person who has an abundance of a trait that we lack. This is the origin of the phrase "opposites attract." In order to appreciate the relationship you are in, or the sort of relationship you seek, it helps to know that patterns exist and that you operate within those patterns. A book such as *Money Harmony* can throw a generous amount of light on the subject, and I recommend reading it to help you through money problems in your marriage.

The Prisoner's Dilemma

Behavioral scientists have spent a considerable amount of time researching a game called the Prisoner's Dilemma. It is a study of the human relationship with cooperation. The basic premise comes from the situation that two suspected crooks are taken into separate rooms for questioning. The crooks have choices. They can support one another in their claims of innocence, or they can inform on the other hoping to get a lighter sentence for themselves. The question in each crook's mind is, "What is my buddy going to say? Should I stay with this relationship, or is it time to bail out?" If they both hold to their claim of innocence, they may both get off. If one turns on the other, the informer gets a lighter sentence, the "sucker" a heavier one. It is a painful dilemma.

The crook metaphor can be extended to include all partners who join forces in risky ventures: lenders and borrowers, teachers and students, employers and employees, unions and management, health insurer and patient, citizen and cop, and not least of all, marriage partners. Each party makes an assessment about the intentions and loyalty of the other player, and based on this assessment either "cooperates" or "defects." If only one defects, the "sucker" is left holding the bag. If both defect, they both suffer.

By cooperating, both win. Defecting is the logical choice in a game that seems to be ending or when one is convinced the partner is not trustworthy.

Extensive statistical study has also shown that cooperation always produces a better outcome than defection over the long term.[26] These studies have also revealed how the value of cooperation can be taught so that cooperation becomes a learned attribute within an organization or group. What this means is that the origins of defection and the path to cooperation are known. Translated into real world terms, the cure for gang violence and all manner of civil strife is known, but it is only taken seriously in the scholastic world.

The problems of drugs, crime, and the helplessness of people on welfare, spring from the fact that many people lack the wholesome pressures commitment brings to bear on them. Without this pressure they fail to discover their capabilities. Without the pressure that comes with motivating relationships they do not have to dig to express their deepest ambitions. As human beings we must participate in a community and submit to its expectations in order to grow and learn.

I see a parallel between the structure of matter as depicted in the working model of the atom, and the structure of society. Atoms have a nucleus and a varying number of electrons that circle this nucleus. Each electron is matched by a proton in the nucleus. The difference between lead and gold, and all other elements, is the number of electrons and protons. In my model I am suggesting that the difference between an alienated, angry, resentful drug dealer in prison, and a kind, productive, mother of three with a college degree and a responsible job, is the number of wholesome commitments she is able to manage. The offender is a crude element that is missing "electrons" or the capacity for commitment. The happy mother has learned and grown as a result of her ability to commit and to submit to a nurturing discipline. Alchemically, we might say that she is gold to the hooligan's lead. Lead is too poisonous to use for water pipes. Gold is so safe and pure that we use it for dental work.

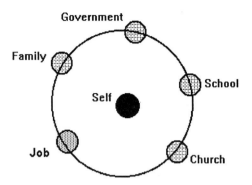

We have the recipe for creating cooperation in America and in the world. The vaccine against hatred exists. Gang problems can be solved. We know how to do it.

The recipe requires a basic understanding of how organizations encourage or prevent exploratory efforts on the part of their members to work together. The more freely cooperative individuals can seek out other individuals in search of partners, the more cooperative alliances are formed. The more aware individuals are of the nature and value of cooperation, the more inclined they are to practice cooperation. Robert Axelrod, Professor of Political Science and Public Policy at the University of Michigan, uses the term "nice" to describe players who never defect first in the game. He proved mathematically the usefulness of being "nice." His research also proved it is costly to the players who are mean or who play with mean players.

Money and mental health

"Almost everyone is uncomfortable talking about money." This is the opening line in the introduction to Olivia Mellan's excellent book, *Money Harmony, Resolving Money Conflicts in Your Life and Relationships*. As a psychotherapist, she has a vantage point that enables her to speak with authority on the subject. Mellan provides lists of questions that help readers get a fix on their point of view and hot buttons about money. She goes on to provide help in neutralizing self-defeating and destructive attitudes.

If you feel that your emotional relationship to money is such that it calls for more reading in search of understanding, I recommend books in the bibliography that will be helpful. If you have great emotional pain about money, you need more than a new set of facts or more advice. You need a program of self-examination and therapy. This is not to say that you are sick, it simply means that you need to identify your attitudes, trace them back to their roots, and establish new expectations of yourself and money. You need a new experience of money, not just talk and ideas.

If you think your problems are severe, or you know someone who has severe problems, a helpful book is Donna Boundy's *When Money is the Drug*. This book deals with compulsions of a rather extreme nature. She cites examples of people who accept struggle and discomfort as a way of life, as "what they deserve," and who shape their finances around this template so that discomfort stays with them. These books, and perhaps some professional counseling are worth considering if your money problems are chronic and your problems recur in a pattern.

Bruce is a power-oriented man who has divorced twice. He uses money as a means of manipulation. When he and Susan divorced in 1989, he felt certain that she would be crawling back to him shortly because she didn't understand money and would squander the divorce settlement. What he didn't count on was how well Susan would learn the lessons of *Wholistic Taxes*. I got Susan as a client because the family's previous joint CPA, Matt, who is still Bruce's CPA, realized he could not impartially advise both Bruce and Susan on the settlement issues.

Bruce has taken Susan to court several times since the divorce on money issues, and there have been several other money issues which have required Susan to hire attorneys. I don't know if their marriage vows made any reference to supporting each other emotionally "whether richer or poorer," but if they did, Bruce certainly broke them. Money, to Bruce, is a means of being the boss.

Susan recalls her attitudes and experiences with money:

We were pretty Ozzie-and-Harriet middle class when I was growing up. There was probably an imbalance in the sense that fun always came first. My parents were probably some of the more irresponsible people about money. Their motto is "Life is short, eat dessert first." I was probably the most responsible of all of us. I was the one out making jewelry to sell. I don't think I had a concept of saving money, or the future. Whatever was there was to be spent. I'm concerned about being independent, not depending on my children. I'm frightened about my own parents eventually depending on me, but they always seem to be doing just fine. I always wonder how they do it.

I really don't remember discussions between my parents about money. My mother worked on and off. Their attitude was, if we wanted a swimming pool, Mom would go to work for the next couple of years. Maybe the first time it hit me that something was out of the priorities was when it was time to go to college, and the money wasn't there. I had to do that myself. Consequently, I only went for a short while. I think I decided then that I would have enough when my kids reached that age.

When I went on my own, which was at 19, I changed as the result of supporting myself. I saved the down payment for a house, which was a long time ago when it was easier. But I put all the money into the house. I didn't think about saving for the future.

Then I met Bruce, and all the control of money was taken away from me. I didn't think about it for the next twenty years. Through the twenty years of our marriage I would handle household expenses, and it was always done the same way. I would pay the bills by writing checks. Then I would make a list of them, and he would give me down to the penny the amount of money to cover the checks I had already written. I never had any extra cash. I now realize that is a strange position to be in, to never have five cents in your checkbook.

When we changed banks I had to go in to the manager and explain that my account would often be overdrawn, and that we would be willing to pay the charges, just don't send any checks back. Most of that time we would average fifty to two-hundred dollars a month in overdraft charges. When I went to the grocery store, they knew me well, so they would let me write a check for an extra twenty dollars. I had a credit card. We didn't want for anything, but there was never to be any money. So that is how I handled money for twenty years.

If I had been involved at all in our financial life when we were married, I would have understood what I understand now. Bruce put himself as sole trustee of the living trust. It allowed him to manipulate our finances. I didn't know that then. Even if you had said, "Susan, Bruce is sole trustee," I would have said, so what? He writes the checks anyway. And it wasn't just Bruce, there were five or six men in that office, the CPA, attorney, stockbroker, the whole group of suits, who let me sign that without saying, "Susan, do you understand?"

I remember making a statement, because they were very serious, and this was fifteen years ago, and I thought it was really funny to say, you know, maybe I ought to get my attorney to look at all of this. I will never forget how many mouths dropped open. They didn't think it was funny. Nobody laughed. My girlfriends laughed when I told them later. And of course I didn't do that. I signed whatever they wanted me to. Now I can see that, of course, that was a disturbing thought to them that I should go find my own attorney and say, should I sign this stuff? That made my life difficult from that point on.

I think for the most part women are not taken seriously by the financial community. That could be part of my paranoia; I'm very used to that. I've been put down for a long time in my marriage and by the people who were important to me. One of the bank managers, in fact the one who called the loan on the house two weeks after the divorce, thought it was funny when they brought me a gift at a football game. It was a really cute black tee shirt, and across the front it said, "I can't be overdrawn, I still have checks left!" And everybody thought that was really funny. What was sad about it is that I wore that and thought it was funny too. I was overdrawn because I never had a penny in my checkbook. It was supposed to be that way. The manager saw that I was overdrawn every month. He must have thought Bruce had the patience of Job. He assumed I was incompetent. After years of it, you start to believe you are incompetent.

As I looked back I began to notice that the file cabinets upstairs were always locked. That should have been a sign to me. Who was he locking them from? Me! Because he handled all of that, because the life style was comfortable, it didn't occur to me that I cared. Actually, I wasn't really interested in those things.

Then all of a sudden here I was going to be on my own and I knew I wouldn't have access to the financial advisors we had used over the years. I went to see Mark, and I didn't know why I was going there. It's just that someone said, "You need a CPA," and I said OK. That is where that started. I was terrified. I expected a CPA to be just a numbers man. I realized that day that this will be OK.

I met Mark and fell apart within five minutes of arriving at his office. I cried through the first two hours of our relationship. That is how frightened I was about it. I saw the money as my security for the rest of my life. I didn't know how much we had, what to do with it, any of those things. Slowly, but surely, Mark helped me a lot. I think I am still very fearful about doing the wrong thing.

Susan has an increasingly self-reliant attitude now. She knows that help is available to her, and she is comfortable asking for it. The transition was difficult for her, but she is managing it well. She is still uncertain, as most people are, where to draw the line between responsible money management and too much spontaneity and playfulness. Her parents, she says, always provide for themselves even though they buy every new gadget that they see and have to have the latest of everything. Susan doesn't know how they do it, and she doesn't discuss it with them. This is a typical situation.

Another story involves a client who bought a piece of property and deliberately avoided discussing the purchase with me, because, he said later, "I might try to talk him out of it." To me this denotes a painful lack of clarity on my client's part as to my role in his affairs. It also denotes a painful lack of clarity of the role of emotions in his own decision-making process. He hides his emotional considerations from me and this is not necessary. I don't challenge his right to be emotional, I just want him to recognize whether his decisions are emotional or logical. I include the emotional aspect of finances in all instances. Often this is as simple as reassuring a client that past actions were sound and well conceived. At times I feel like a teacher awarding a well-deserved "A" on a student's paper.

Finding common ground

My theory of marriage is that a couple needs enough similarities between them to make marriage possible, and enough differences to make it interesting. Too much similarity, and they quickly begin to take each other for granted. It also suggests that one of them is doing all the thinking. Too much difference, and they face great challenges sharing activities, goals, and friends. The overlap in interests and values provides common ground. This common ground is essential in a harmonious money relationship.

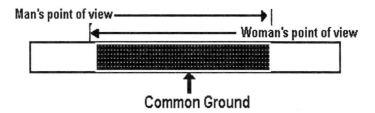

If each partner can appreciate half of the other's domain, this brings the total size of common ground to 50 percent of the material in the relationship. Unless one or both partners is harboring compulsive tendencies that derail common sense, 50 percent shared space is ample for solving most problems, including most financial problems.

A hundred percent shared space, even if theoretically possible, hardly seems pleasant. It would render one of the partner's redundant and irrelevant. Anyone who does not contribute something unique to a relationship has no real investment in the relationship. In real life it often happens that partners differ in their money management attitudes and skills. These differences may produce stability, as in the case of savers pairing up with spenders. They can also produce chaos as when spenders pair up with other spenders. This is consistent with the premise that a partnership needs enough differences between the two points of view.

I know of several excellent books that specialize in the area of marriage for those who feel they would benefit from such study. I am firmly convinced that all marriages benefit from periodic reading and counseling. These activities freshen and tune-up a relationship. I particularly recommend Harville Hendrix's books, my favorite being *Getting the Love you Want*. I also find John Gray's *Men Are From Mars, Women Are From Venus* helpful.

A book that may seem unrelated, but isn't, is *Staying Well With The Gentle Art of Verbal Self-Defense* by Suzette Hayden Elgin. This book teaches the fine art of listening for meaning. It is a bit scholarly in places, but no one says you have to read every page.

The pressures of marriage, or any other profound commitment, for that matter, force us to do things that lead to discoveries about ourselves. Pressure leads to the recognition of resources that would have remained dormant, had we not needed them to cope with a crisis. The crises we face are often of our own making as deep instincts work their will through our worldly affairs.

How candid are you?

The candor matrix is a litmus test for your degree of sharing in areas of money and information about money. There are no correct answers. I agree with advocates of the 12-step programs that we are only as sick as our secrets. The fewer secrets we keep because of fear of embarrassment, the healthier we are.

Fill out the candor matrix and feel it for hot spots. When you feel resistance, you are near sources of strong opinions. These are decision points, the pivot points for the direction your life goes. Knowing where these decision points are is key to self-understanding.

The candor matrix is revealing when people who are closely

related fill it out separately and then compare results. Assign a number from one to ten to indicate how easily you can discuss these topics with the various relationships in your life. You may equate difficult with inappropriate. Best same-sex friend is meant to be your best friend apart from your mate or significant other. If your mate is same-sex, then choose your best friend who is not your mate.

The candor matrix

The candor matrix--what you discuss and with whom				
Rate 1-10, 10 is most difficult or least appropriate	Kids	Parents	Spouse	Best friend (not spouse)
Your annual income				
Your fears about money				
Your will or trust				
Your kids' college expenses				
Asking for a cash loan				
Offering a cash loan				
Discussing their delinquent debt to you				
How they handle money				
Your ability to budget				
Explaining your loss that they predicted				
Totals				

You can create a graphic representation of your results using the grid on the next page if you like.

	Kids	Parents	Spouse	Friend
100				
90				
80				
70				
60				
50				
40				
30				
20				
10				

Do you and your mate have separate checking accounts or a joint account, or both? Why? Why not do it differently? Men often want joint accounts to express their desire to share. It is a form of bonding. Women often prefer separate accounts for a measure of privacy. There is no right way, but it is important to be aware of your preferences and those of your mate in order to facilitate the engineering and design of your overall money management plan. The point is to notice the differences in your value systems and the uniqueness of your tastes and preferences.

Money also has an effect on people, its own influence, so to speak. At least one study shows that increased prosperity corresponds with increased marital infidelity. Infidelity at $20,000 annual income was 30 percent for men, and it rose to 70 percent at $60,000 and more. Money increases sex appeal. It makes sexual variety more accessible with less investment of time and intrigue on the man's part.

Staying Together

Money can pull relationships apart. I have seen too many couples lose their relationship because one or both of the partners has gone in pursuit of money. From February 1 until April 15, I schedule my work from 10:00 a.m. to midnight. I get up in time to have breakfast with my family.

Len has been a client for about eight years. He commuted from San Diego to Los Angeles. He and his wife maintained a home in San Diego because they had several rental properties to supervise. He spent the week in L.A., and big chunks of their evenings together were devoted to tending to business. They divorced about four years ago. It was due in part to the amount of time they were separated.

Money and gender

I will content myself by making the broad assertion that the entry of women in politics has raised the tone of the body politic wherever it has been adopted.
—Joseph Howell, May 1915

My great grandfather wrote eloquently on the subject of women voting. He was an enthusiastic and outspoken supporter of it. It seems odd that there was any question about whether women were competent to vote. Still, women are judged less competent in business today by many who would deny it publicly. I see women every week who lack an edge to their self-confidence because friends and family have convinced them of imaginary inadequacies.

About 60 percent of my clients are women. Many are referred by people in support groups for women who are recently divorced. Many of these women have not managed money before. Their ex-husbands did it all. They feel cast adrift.

I don't have a lot of divorces in my practice. I try to talk clients out of divorce. This may not seem to be any of my business as a CPA, but it is not such a great leap to discuss divorce with people I have known for years after advising them on so personal a subject as their finances.

I have three women as clients who were married to powerful

men who largely controlled their lives but neglected or mishandled their financial needs. All three were essentially cast adrift when they divorced. Susan and Nan's husbands were businessmen, Jane was married to an accountant. After the divorce these women had to learn about money from the ground up after decades of being insulated from reality. I urge people in this situation to put their money in some place safe like a passbook savings account until they are confident that they can make informed decisions in their own behalf.

Money and dominance, the gender difference

In India, a cow is a creature that can parade itself through a village of starving Hindu people, calm in the certainty that they deem the cow sacred and will therefore not carve it up and roast it. It is not news that men are sacred cows in boardrooms across America, calm in the knowledge that their entrenched power protects them from accountability for largely excluding women from their ranks.

Ironically, the famous *Barron's* Roundtable, an annual gathering of ten of the world's savviest investors, who nearly always are men, is selected by two people, one of whom is a woman. Kate Welling, the woman in question, was quoted by John Rothchild in *Worth* as saying that this is a "very sexist gathering." A vicious circle sustains this arrangement, and since *Wholistic Taxes* is an examination of how to break vicious circles, it makes sense to spend a moment with this example.

There are at least 4,000 mutual funds in the United States, the exact number depending on what day of the week you count them. According to Rothchild, women manage a tiny fraction of them, in the neighborhood of 12 percent. Yet, he concludes, "taken as a group, over the last three years, funds managed by women have outperformed funds managed by men or by committee." So why do so few women get the opportunity to prove themselves? Rothchild thinks the successes of women are viewed as flukes, novelties. Too many people think that if you want serious advice, you should talk to a man.

Working mates

Working mates often get to keep about half of what they earn in gross pay. Let's assume that one spouse can cover all living costs. The second spouse, lacking deductible expenses which are all paid by the first spouse, typically pays 28 percent federal, 8 percent state, 7.65 percent Social Security, 1 percent disability for a total of about 45 percent. If working creates a cost for child care and commuting, the cost of working becomes more than half the worker's gross pay. It only makes sense to evaluate the job and the time it takes in the light of the net pay it generates.

Marlene became annoyed when I explained this concept to her. She confided in me that she was contributing to deductible expenses with money from her income, yet her husband was taking all the deductions. Since he was earning triple her income, he apparently felt the deductions were better applied to his tax return. It taught me that I had to be careful how I presented these ideas since the information sometimes came as a big surprise to my client. She was startled to learn that her income was being whittled down so severely by taxes, and in a sense her deductible expenses were in vain.

Dominance in the family

Many times I have seen money divided into yours, mine, and ours. Often the wife supports the husband through his education or professional apprenticeship, only to be held hostage to money after things get going financially. Mildred had some money from an inheritance. Her husband George paid the household bills, but demanded that Mildred's discretionary spending had to come from her inheritance. He took the position that the rest of his income was his and that he did not have to account for it in any way. He used money as an offensive weapon.

Fathers have abandoned wives and children since time began. Mythological Chronos ate his, though they remained alive and were spat out later, seemingly no worse for the wear. They went on with their eternal lives as gods, perhaps wiser for their experience. On the human scale this abandonment is felt as tragedy with all its attendant pain.

I would like to see our government repeal all laws that discourage marriage. I would like to see couples get counseling when they need it to achieve fairness and gentleness where money is concerned in their relationship.

I would like to see citizens express their feelings on legislation to our elected officials, and their feelings on money harmony in marriage to their spouse.

Chapter Nine: Parents Becoming Grandparents

As fall approached, Dad and Mother became increasingly concerned about the lack of medical facilities for the coming birth of the baby. We moved to Huntsville and rented a vacant, almost-abandoned, log cabin from Uncle Louis's brother, and Dad went in search of work. He found a job at the Franklin County Sugar Company in Whitney, Idaho, shovelling stinking beet pulp out of a deep fermentation pit into farmers' wagons for ten cents per ton. Gordon was born in Hunstville on November 16, 1922 but Dad could not come because he was threatened with loss of his job if he took time off to see the baby.

—Roy Howard Maughan, 1913-1992

Desiderata is one of my favorite sources of inspiration. The name means "things that are desirable." It advises us to surrender gracefully the things of youth. This is hard to do when the emphasis in our culture is predominantly on the pleasures and privileges of youth.

When baby boomers get old, we will be the largest group of village elders ever. If for no other reason than our sheer numbers, it is important that we learn to do it with style. It is time to prepare to be responsible, interesting, exciting village elders who will affirm the joys of patience, individuality, and personal integrity. We need to be good examples for the next generation.

We can draw inspiration from people like Bill Bell. When he was 71 he competed in his 14th iron man event in Hawaii. To add to the irony, this was the first time he won in his age group. Storms kicked up ocean currents off the coast of the Hawaiian island of Kona where the event was held, but he pressed on to the finish. Bell faced head winds and 80 degree temperatures during the bike race segment of the competition. When he finished, he told reporters: "I didn't turn in any personal best times, but I've never felt better or stronger than I did in this race."

We need a more positive attitude toward old age because most of us face increasing amounts of it. The insurance industry tells us that the average man lives 19 years past his 65 year retirement age. Women live 22 years past 65. The government will not be kind to you either. The taxes on Social Security put retired people in a disproportionately high tax bracket compared to the population at large.

Even with our present wariness of old age we can view "not losing" as a form of winning. If you enter retirement without major losses in quality of life, that is a victory, as far as I am concerned. Quality of life in retirement rests primarily on ample funds and sound health. To enhance our respect for our later years, I prescribe an examination of history to learn what it has to offer in the way of perspective and a respect for durability.

My aunt, Mary Ellen Stoddard Smith, published a series of accounts about our family. One of these hardcover volumes runs 350 pages and begins with the birth of Joseph Howell, my great grandfather, on February 17, 1857 in Utah. His grandson later wrote about him and is quoted in the book. Joseph married one of my ancestors, Mary Elizabeth Maughan on October 24, 1878. It is recorded that Mary's beautiful blonde hair was so fascinating to the local indians that they offered to buy her several times. The book, which is titled *From Wales To Washington*, traces in considerable detail the accomplishments, trials, and adventures of the people who spawned me.

One passage in Joseph's account particularly strikes me:

May 28, 1906. More than two years has

elapsed since I made my last entry in this book, but tonight in reading of the incidents recorded then I am strikingly impressed with the interest that time invests even the most common place matters, when we recall them. In the ordinary Course of our daily routine, we sometimes feel, that there is nothing eventful enough to be worthy of record, and we pass along without marking it. This tendency is certainly a grave mistake, which is the more impressed upon me by a perusal of the few incidents I jotted down, when I first conceived the idea of keeping a diary of my public career, but alas two years have intervened of perhaps the most eventful period of my life, without any record being recorded by me. I am keenly sensible this evening of my neglect and have again resolved to take up the duty of making a record of daily events in my various environments.

It reminds me that today we consider the past expendable, a minor curiosity. Much is lost by that. When we take photographs, we call them "snapshots." *Snap*, according to the dictionary, is to sever suddenly or with a snapping sound. It probably refers to the noise a camera shutter makes. It also reflects the hasty way that we "break off" an impression of the world around us and stuff it into the camera. Most snapshots are taken so far from the subject it is difficult to tell who or what it is. The center of interest is often at the edge of the picture. We hurry too much. We don't notice what our eyes are telling us.

Many of us never date or properly file these snapshots. Careful photographers speak of "making" a photograph. That contemplative approach enables us to experience the subject matter, to merge our attention with it. Such an approach to our lives reveals the texture of it to us. It brings our attention to the fact that the detail of our lives matters. I like the philosophy of Buddhism that teaches nothing is important, but everything matters.

As we live longer our relationship with retirement and with retired people changes. Parents used to die, on average, while their children were still working. Nowadays, you might sit retired in a rocking chair on a the same front porch with your parents, and reminisce together about your careers. The *Orange County Register* recently published an account of a 70-year-old man who threw a 73rd wedding anniversary party for his 94-year-old father and his 92-year-old mother. These situations will become more common.

In 1989 *Modern Maturity* magazine had a circulation of 20,314,462 making it the most widely read magazine in America. This segment of the population will be large for many years to come because the baby boomers will be the biggest generation to retire so far.

Social Security is being nibbled away

Social Security became law in August of 1935. It paid out about $325,000,000,000 in 1994. The average retirement benefit was $674 per month, $8,088 per year. If all of the approximately 250,000,000 people in this country, counting retired people themselves, children, prisoners, and the unemployed, contributed to today's Social Security bill, it would cost each of us about $1,300 per year. Working people each pay more than this. The tragedy is that each worker's Social Security contributions are used to pay current benefits. The actuarial tables predict bankruptcy within a few decades.

In 1989, fifteen percent of Americans received Social Security payments. One-fifth of the people living in Florida were on Social Security that year, and the figure was nearly as high in West Virginia and Arkansas, which ranked second and third respectively measured by percentage of citizens receiving the checks. With the swelling ranks of old people, the system is much too expensive to be viable, and everyone knows it. The government is tightening its grip on Social Security in many ways.

Certified Financial Planner Dion Collins, born in 1959, asks his clients whether they want Social Security included in his calculations for their retirement plans. He estimates that 80 percent or more of his clients opt to ignore Social Security for the purposes of making their retirement projections.

Congress prepared an unpleasant surprise for retired taxpayers on Social Security to discover early in 1995 when they filed their 1994 income tax returns. In certain situations, people found that a $1.00 increase in earnings resulted in an increase in taxable income of $1.85. It used to be that Social Security income was tax free, and people planned their retirements based on the assumption that it would remain tax free. The tax-free status ended for Social Security income received in 1991 when half of Social Security income became subject to tax. Up to 85 percent of Social Security benefits received in 1994 is subject to income tax. Married people filing jointly with an income above $44,000 and single people making $34,000 will find that 85 percent of their income from Social Security is taxable. An income of $32,000 for a married couple filing jointly makes 50 percent of Social Security income taxable.

Income from tax-free municipal bonds and other sources can render this accounting picture extremely complex. This is a situation that calls for professional tax guidance. In the past this transaction was simple, and the taxpayer could easily make the necessary calculations. Thanks to repeated tax "simplifications" you now need to hire a professional.

Until 1994, taxes on Social Security were on the first 50 percent of benefits. Two single people can earn up to $68,000 before they enter the bracket where 85 percent of Social Security is subject to tax, but a married couple enters this bracket at $44,000. It is another marriage penalty the government has imposed on Americans.

Here is an example of this complicated calculation. Let us say that part-time work brings in $15,000, tax-free municipal bonds bring in $5,000, and Social Security brings in $12,000. Divide the Social Security income by two, and add it to the other sources. In this scenario, $1,000 of Social Security income is subject to tax. Prior to 1991 this $1,000 of Social Security income would not have been taxed.

"Tax free" now becomes more of a figure of speech to the

extent that tax-free income pushes total income, called "provisional" income by the IRS, into higher brackets. Your tax-free municipal bonds combine with your previously tax-free Social Security income to put you in a bracket where you must pay taxes on as much as 85 percent of your Social Security benefits. The IRS requires that owners of IRA accounts begin to draw them down no later than 70 and 1/2 years of age. Naturally, there are penalties for anyone who does not comply. The government makes money where it can.

Retirement plans

You are over 40. We know that because you're reading this ad, and people under 40 generally can't be bothered to read an ad about retirement.
—Advertisement in *Worth* magazine

Retire, according to Webster's dictionary, means to draw back, to go away to a secluded place, to retreat from action. Retirement is not for everyone. The idea of retirement at age 65 is a relative novelty in the saga of human development. It is a notion that arose from the abundance made possible by the industrial revolution, and it didn't really catch on in its present form until the last few decades. It was only recently that retirement became symbolized by tanned couples dressed all in white, gamboling across lush fairways and basking on tropical beaches as a full time occupation.

It is an idea that will be severely tested if 76,000,000 baby boomers decide to climb into the retirement boat. More likely, the whole definition of retirement will be revised right down to its roots. Business magazines have already begun publishing articles that explore new definitions of work and retirement, and these pioneering essays mark the beginning of widespread revisions of our expectations about these subjects.

When President Roosevelt set retirement at 65, the average American lived 63 years. In 1937, when Social Security was launched, there were 40 people working to support each retired recipient. The maximum contribution was $30 per year. Now there are three workers for each Social Security recipient, and the maximum contribution for 1993 was $3,757.

Experts predict that in the year 2020 retired people will equal the number of working people. It will literally become a matter of "how the other half lives."

It is clear that the Social Security approach to retirement is an anachronism. It is dead, and it only waits for a puff of wind to knock it over. The answer is a fundamental restructuring of the idea of retirement. It includes taking more personal responsibility for saving, especially with instruments such as 401 (k) plans. Currently fewer than half the baby boomers who are eligible for such plans participate in them. Not all who do participate are sufficiently aggressive.

We have to redefine the concept of employment. We have to examine our talents, skills, and interests and adapt the ways in which we use them as we get older. The main reason for retiring at 65 in the past might have been physical incapacity. Now we are healthier longer, and work is much less dependent on physical strength, or even mobility. The electronic workplace has made work accessible to a much wider range of people as measured by wellness and strength than ever before. Work today involves toting that barge and lifting that bale less and less often. Given these changes, we are capable of working much longer than previous generations.

Coming out on top

In how many areas of life do you rank in the top 3 percent in terms of achievement? You may be surprised at how easy it is to win a place in this small, elite group at retirement. To place in the top 3 percent in terms of retirement income (apart from Social Security and wages) you only need to derive $20,000 per year, $1,666 per month, $384.61 per week, from your retirement plan and investments. The median average income for an American in retirement after 45 years of labor is $5,500 per year, or $105.76

per week. The reason it is so easy is that your peers are performing so poorly.

The explanation for this widespread and genuinely sad scenario is that Americans have not learned to set and live with financial priorities. I recommend that you write a letter to your present self from the perspective of where you will be ten years into your retirement. Write a letter back in time describing the future. Your first question is what age will you be ten years into retirement? Will you be 65? 75? 100?

If you are like me, you will make it a rosy future. The financial goal I recommend is an income of $20,000 per year (as measured in 1994 dollars). Be more generous with yourself if that is your nature. Then reminisce about some of the great moves that led up to this future. Thank yourself. Congratulate yourself. Be specific about the things you did right along the way. Reinforce your good decisions. This method of anticipation sets up a level of heightened expectation that makes what you are doing now seem more worthwhile. Stephen Covey teaches that it is fundamental to success to see the end result we want from the time we take our first step. I encourage you to set this book down and write the letter from your future now.

> **Premise #7 of Wholistic Taxes:**
> **Intentions produce greater results**
> **when committed to writing.**

Social Security

Social Security is a rip off in several ways. First, it is in truth a disguised form of income tax. The money does not go into a fund that awaits the taxpayer at retirement, it goes to pay current operating expenses of the government. Second, it is an income tax that applies to the first dollars earned. This means it hits poor and middle income people the hardest. The more the income tax burden is transferred to Social Security, the more the modest earner gets burned. Third, the money will not be there. Current estimates (and estimates have consistently been too optimistic) predict that the Social Security fund will grind to a close by the year 2029. Isolated efforts to save the fund, or prolong its life, include limiting a drug addicts' access to cash payments for 36 months from the time they entered treatment.

Contemporary financial thinking favors 401 (k) plans as an alternative to Social Security. This does not mean that the government will let you withdraw from the Social Security program and redirect your money as you choose, but it does provide a savings method that will work to your benefit, unlike Social Security.

Social Security began as a one percent tax on the first $3,000 of income. When you got the money back, after retirement began, it was tax free. Now the government takes 6.2 percent of the first $62,700 (1996 limit), and uses the money that doesn't go out immediately to retired people to pay bills. There is *no* Social Security reserve fund. The law requires that Social Security surpluses be invested in Treasury securities. Treasury securities are a form of federal debt. Senator Daniel Moynihan argued that the 1989 deficit was distorted by $52,000,000,000 in this manner. The money isn't really there.

Social Security is important to a lot of people. The government estimates that retired people get 38 percent of their income from it. Savings and investments provide another 28 percent. I find it revealing that savings are smaller than Social Security, given the puny amount of Social Security people receive.

FICA, a term familiar to most Americans from their paycheck stubs, records the employee's contributions to Social Security and Medicare. Before 1994, Social Security was billed at 6.2 percent of the employee's income on the first $60,600 of income.

Effective with earnings in 1994, there is no upper limit for Medicare deductions. Does this removal of the upper limit change anything? It does to Wayne Gretzky. Gretzky's 1994 contract with the Kings is worth $8.5 million per year. Mr. Gretzky pays $123,250 of that to Medicare, and the Kings match that amount as a payroll tax. Now you might argue that in a high-risk line of work such as ice hockey, he might get substantial benefit someday from Medicare. The government does not charge this tax only to athletes and daredevils. It charges everyone. You don't have to make $8.5 million per year to feel the burden of this tax.

Mistakes favor Uncle Sam

Government prefers complexity to simplicity. IRA funds can be withdrawn without penalty beginning at the age of 59 1/2 years. Why not 59 or 60 years? The government mandates that withdrawals begin by age 70 1/2. Why not 70 or 71 years? Lawmakers, many of whom are lawyers, have an exaggerated affinity for complexity, probably because it makes their services necessary.

A prime example is the tax form for calculating Passive Loss Limitation. Calculations must be carried to six decimal places. A computer is all but essential in preparing such a document, especially since a change in one figure requires changes to the rest of them. These are painfully laborious forms. I gained more than a dozen new clients who formerly calculated their own taxes, but who could not, or would not cope with this one new form.

The government wants you to make mistakes so that it can profit from them. It complicates IRA regulations with that goal in mind. If you retire or leave a company that pays you your retirement funds, the government withholds 20 percent of that amount. The rationale is that there is going to be a tax on this money, so the government has an advance on the amount due. The problem for the individual is that if his intention is roll that money into an IRA rollover account, he now has only 80 percent of his money. There is now a tax liability on the 20 percent the government took. In order to rollover the entire amount, you would have to make up the missing 20 percent out of other funds.

The government has no intention of changing this. I attended a satellite seminar at which Bill Bradley, U.S. senator from New Jersey, answered a question on that subject with the declaration that the IRS expects to impose substantial penalties because of taxpayers' lack of awareness of the law. Subsequently, the government made it a corporate responsibility to inform employees of the proper way to handle these funds, so penalties have been much less than expected initially.

The solution is to have the check made out to the plan administrator of the new IRA fund. Don't touch the money yourself if you want to avoid the IRS hassle and become a candidate for their penalty. The IRA maneuver is an extension of what the government calls "back up withholding" which is what happens if you win a large sum gambling. The casino will withhold 20 percent or more from your winnings and will send that amount to the IRS before it passes through your hands.

Individual Retirement Accounts, or IRAs are a better system for providing for retirement needs than counting on Social Security. The government can't seem to leave well enough alone, given that Americans need to be trained to save. They need incentives to save. Passbook savings accounts, which are currently paying interest on the order of 2.5 percent, which is subsequently taxed, do not provide an incentive to save money from an investment point of view. Such savings are superior to cash in the cookie jar only from the perspective that bank accounts are covered by insurance.

IRAs were designed so that each individual could deposit up to $2,000 per year and defer the taxes on both the amount invested and the interest it earned until the money was taken out of the IRA. This arrangement quickly became too generous in the eyes of government. Now, since 1986, if *either* of two married people are covered by a pension plan, *neither* can deduct their IRA allocations from their taxable income if they earn more than $50,000 combined. It is, in effect, another form of marriage penalty. The earnings remain tax-deferred, but to a young person, the reward seems incredibly remote. The reward of a lowered tax bill the following April for this year's contribution is an incentive to a person 25 years old. The reward of deferred taxes on earnings that will not be available to spend for 34 1/2 more years inspires very few people to act. The government made another bad decision when they decided to reduce the incentives to establish IRAs. Proof of the government's <u>ability to discourage</u> and prevent IRA contributions is that the number of returns showing an IRA fell 73 percent from 1985 to 1991.

Basically the government has taken the position that it will make it difficult for citizens to provide for themselves. A 1994 change to the Qualified Plan Compensation Limitation means that the contribution to a retirement fund is now limited to $22,500 per year, or 15 percent of $150,000. The previous limit was $30,000 per year, or 15 percent of $200,000. The government seems to want your taxes right away. This nation, founded in 1776, cannot wait until this generation retires to get its money.

Pensions

A headline in the December 6, 1994 *Los Angeles Times* said, "U.S. Pension Plan Deficit Grows 35 percent to $71 Billion." Reporter Kathy Kristof explained that 8,000,000 workers are at risk because of poor investment returns. Hardest hit are workers in steel, auto, tire and airline industries. A new law bars companies from using "dubious accounting techniques to make their plans seem healthier than they are." We need more corporate honesty. We need companies that promote people based on honesty.

Passing on wealth

First I give and Bequeath to My Wife Cecelia Morgans Sole Executrix to have the full Controul of all My Property Real, Personal and Monies Goods and Chattels of what nature or Kind soever So long as She lives or Remains My Widow but at her death or Marrige The said Property real Personal or Monies Goods and Chattels of what nature or kind Soever to be Equally devided amongst the following Individuals To share and Share Alike.

—From the will of Morgan Morgan, 1879, filed in Tooele County, Utah, reproduced just as he wrote it.

My ancestor Morgan Morgan lived another ten years after signing his last will and testament, and the record shows that he wrote it while in good health. I applaud him for his planning. With the complexity that has developed since he passed away, it makes increasingly good sense to plan your affairs as he did.

Nowadays, it typically costs about 30 to 40 percent of an estate's value to settle an estate that is transferred by means of a will, although there have been famous cases of losses of 70 percent and more. Humphrey Bogart's estate shrank by 30 percent, which amounted to $274,234, for example. Walt Disney's 30 percent shrinkage came to $6,811,943. This shrinkage is a combination of taxes and legal fees.

There are ways to reduce both, while also reducing much of the frustration and delay that can accompany probate. Probate costs between 5 and 10 percent of the estate's value and proceeds on a time table determined by the court. It might move quickly, or it might drag out for months or years. Probate fees are based on the gross value of your estate. If you have a million dollar estate with debts that consume 90 percent of it, probate fees are still based on the full million. If probate costs 10 percent, your heirs would get nothing in that scenario. It is good to avoid probate.

Living trusts have many advantages over wills. They avoid probate and the generous fees that come with that. Living trusts may be more expensive to initiate, but they are a good value in terms of inheritance tax reduction. Congress seems eager to whittle away at the potential savings from living trusts as compared to wills, but as of this writing the difference is significant. It is worth investigating for this and other advantages which include the ease with which a trustee can take over the affairs of a person who is incapacitated.

Educating parents

Dorothy, now four years into retirement, says that when she was growing up it wasn't considered polite to talk about money. As I mention in another chapter, Dorothy lost heavily through bad investments, partly because she failed to ask the right questions of her advisor. This old fashioned notion of propriety proved to be painfully expensive for her.

Will is 82 and lives in a rambling old house that he cannot afford to maintain. He putters in a garden far too large for his level of energy and fitness. He built the home from scratch 27 years ago, and it has no mortgage. His wife is bedridden and lives in a convalescent home from which she has no prospect of returning. Their adult son still lives in the family home.

Will can't bear the thought of selling the place because his whole sense of self and security is psychologically connected to the house. His boldest move in terms of planning is an old fashioned will, with its expensive features of probate and estate taxes. He isn't comfortable talking about these money issues, nor his own demise, and he becomes withdrawn and sullen at any mention of estate planning. Will's situation and the emotional pain he is experiencing are all too common.

Will could transfer his home equity to his four children as gifts in increments of $10,000 per year if he chose, or of $20,000 per year if his wife matched the gift. There is no tax on gifts until they exceed that amount per calendar year. (As an aside, be sure to document gifts. If you write a check it should be deposited in time to clear the bank before the new year starts in order to leave the new year clear for another gift to that recipient.) Done properly, this eliminates inheritance taxes on the amount transferred during his life time. He does not do that because such a move would be an acknowledgment of his own mortality, and he is not equal to that task.

Will has not investigated a living trust. If he did, he would discover that it is a fairly straightforward document. Most of them are much easier to read than the typical legal document. Two factors make them difficult from an emotional standpoint, however. First, they don't save the parents any money at all. The cost of establishing a living trust is usually in the $1,000 to $2,000 range. Second, you have to face your own mortality. Obviously the second consideration is a major hurdle for Will to overcome for estate planning purposes.

In the new millennium we will, of necessity, rekindle our respect for old age. Retirement will not be taken for granted. It will be more of an individual decision. We will be far less dependent on employers or the government to fund our retirement if we do take one. We have to develop a more receptive attitude toward being old. It is time that we learn to appreciate it.

There are many stories of people retiring after busy careers only to find that the lack of structure disturbed them. Some lose their health. For others the only path is to return to work of some kind. It is usually better to remain active, though the nature of the activity can change. For some people this is a time to return to family activities with grandchildren, or to travel, or to learn to paint.

My grandmother, Eldora Johnson Maughan, began to paint at the age of 70. She promised a painting to each of her heirs. When she passed away at the age of 92 she had painted more than 250 works and given them to family members. She died a great, great, great grandmother. She had 70-year-old children, and they had produced a long line of recipients for her paintings.

It is a service to our parents to make it as easy as possible for them to discuss money with us. Those of us who competed with our parents, or who harbor any resentments are likely to find this task difficult. It is an act of mercy to open the door to friendly discussions of money. It can result in greater financial security and peace of mind for all concerned.

We will all, with a bit of luck, be old some day. It is well to make close our relationships with our elders in order to learn as much about the role as possible for the day when we will need to play it ourselves.

Chapter Ten: Money and Your Children

Dear Daughter Barbara,

We have derived much comfort and joy in reading the letters we have recently received in more liberal number from our loved ones at home but none of them has breathed a purer holy affection than yours. Your kind and loving sentiments fill our hearts with gratitude and tenderness toward you. We greatly rejoiced to learn that you had arrived home in safety and that you are secure in the House of your friends, yea more than friends, you are under the care and protection of a large circle of loving relatives, who will all keenly sense your situation and be ready and willing to provide for your comfort and pleasure.

—Joseph Howell to his daughter, August 2, 1913

Where did you learn about money? Reach beyond techniques to underlying assumptions about money. How was the concept of "enough" conveyed in your family? What was it like to ask your parents for money? What were conversations like between your parents when they discussed money? Was money the subject of arguments in your house? Did you have any close relatives who were much richer or poorer than the family in general? How were these relatives treated and how did they treat you?

While we know of the pressure money creates in this world,

our school system does little to prepare students for the realities they will face. Many successful adults are getting no financial advice at all. They see a tax preparer briefly once a year, and that is the extent of their money management efforts. Even prosperous people who pay for and receive expensive advice are frequently advised badly. One example of such advice is to choose poor investments as the lesser of two evils. It makes no sense to me to spend money that would have gone for taxes to buy something useless in order to avoid paying Uncle Sam, yet that is what many people do when they pay mortgage interest.

What are your children learning in high school about money? I called my local high school district, which includes six high schools. Two of the six schools have a class titled Personal Management, which might, I was told, include something about money management. The only other class dealing with money among these six schools is a class on economics. Economics is the macro, or big picture view of money, and has little relevance to personal attitudes and handling of budgets. If you are counting on the school system to provide children with an understanding of money, you will be disappointed.

Our society is overly concerned with rights and negligent of responsibilities. Our school system needs broad-based support in teaching responsibility to our children.

This generation of children growing up today is the first to be raised by parents who have no experience of the Great Depression of 1929. We, the baby boom generation born after the end of World War II, learned about it secondhand from our parents. My father was seven years old when the stock market crashed, signalling the beginning of the Depression. Our grandparents dealt with the Depression as adults. My grandfather was 38 at the time. Baby boomers only know stories about the Depression, and we will convey essentially no emotional content about it whatsoever to children. We have the facts, but not the experiences. We know that the crash of 1929 and the crash of 1987 involved similar amounts of money. The difference was that during the earlier crash, investors were buying on margins of ten percent. Now an investor must have

50 percent of the money required for a purchase before making a commitment. In addition, margin accounts are less popular. Perhaps three percent of my clients have margin accounts.

We might do better if we learned more from the past. We might do better if we examined our beliefs in more detail and traced the paths by which they entered our thinking. Often our impressions are formed so early that we no longer recognize them as personal values. They are so ancient that we come to think of them as part of our basic nature rather than as something we came to believe as we were growing up. My client Robert was raised in a family where both hillbilly-rustic and aspiring-suburban-chic were present. Advocates of both positions resented and feared the other. In his words,

> Grandma heated her house with a wood stove. She had indoor plumbing, but you were only allowed to use it if you were sick, otherwise you went out to a building we called the gonnaker. One year Uncle Ole built a new outhouse and named it 'Rilla's Roost' in honor of grandma, whose name was Arrilla. Her washing machine had wringers to squeeze the clothes dry enough to hang them on the line.

> This was not so long ago. She died in 1969, the same year Neil Armstrong walked on the moon. In the early sixties Dad and I lived in an all-white, suburban neighborhood and did things that weren't trendy yet such as drinking wine. Dad wore custom-made suits and drove a Lincoln Continental.

> The two worlds seemed congenial to me, but the division between them seemed to bother other people. That part of it was unsettling to me. Dad was obsessed with differentiating himself from the rustic ways of his family, and I copied his sense of panic. The underlying assumption was that the panic was a necessary part of the formula.

The Glover family

Walter Glover was one of many returning GIs after World War II. He and his wife Lois found housing in short supply. As he says, you had to know somebody who would move you to the head of the list in order to get a place to rent.

He didn't have connections, so he bought a lot and built a house using a Cal-Vet loan. The house was 850 square feet, and it did not please his neighbors to have it on their street. He also bought a 1948 Chevrolet convertible for $2,600. He still chides himself for this luxury. "It was a show car. It was loaded," he reminisces. "We could have put that money into equities of some kind. Think what that money would be today in a good, solid mutual fund."

"You wouldn't have had as much fun," Lois reminds him.

Although their home is large and well built, to this day Walt's cars are the only conspicuous display of wealth to be seen. He has a classic Mercedes sports car and a new Cadillac. "I'm fairly conservative," Walter says. "She's super conservative," he says of his wife. "She's looking at the matter of not depending on anyone else once she's alone. It was a big fear in my mother's life since she was an only child. She was very fearful that she was going to have somebody take care of her.

"In 1930 I was seven. I knew my dad was out of work and having trouble finding a job. Anybody who was old enough to understand the situation in the years of the Depression has never forgotten it. It left me with a gnawing fear that I had to get to the next level, so I went to college. That left a heck of an impression.

"Another thing that left an impression on me was when my dad finally got employed in 1935. He took a civil service job with the Department of Water and Power. I think he was getting paid $25 a month and living away from home up in Mono County. Boy, he hung onto that job! He was in his early 40s, and you couldn't have got him to leave that job for anything unless somebody guaranteed him a lifelong income.

"He worked seven days a week to accumulate time off. He came home for one week each month after working 21 days straight. He did that for five years before he got a transfer so that he could live at home again.

"The thing that made an impression on me," Walter says, "is that he hated the job. He just hated it. He hated to get up in the morning. I said, hey, that's not for me. I'm going to do something I enjoy."

The Glovers invested early in real estate. Their four children were recruited to work on these properties, which were used for rental income. The four children all reacted differently to the work.

"I think everyone that has more than one kid marvels at how each winds up so different," Walter observes. He comments that he was 25 when his first child was born.

"What do you know about raising kids at that age? Nothing. Absolutely nothing," he says. Walter and Lois passed along to their children what they knew best: discipline and self-control. First-born son Terry picked up their ideas and went on to share investments with his parents.

Second-born Dennis was a late bloomer, financially speaking, buying his first house after "scraping enough together to put down on a house they had been renting," as Walter puts it. "It was kind of late in life. One of the first things we did was to own. Our thought was, no matter how small it is, let's build some equity.

"That's one thing we impressed on the kids, don't be afraid of hard work." The Glovers tried allowances and discovered "they weren't very successful." They were tied to the fulfillment of chores, and the chores were not always completed. Walt says he instead encouraged his children to find jobs.

The Glovers have planned thoroughly in regard to passing on their estate. An insurance policy will cover estate taxes. The money to pay the premium is given as a gift to the elder son, so there are is no tax due on it.

Not only do times change, so each generation's interpretation changes as values are passed down. Copying the previous generation's methods of dealing with money and children is likely to be only marginally successful. This is because conditions do not repeat themselves. For better or worse, we must invent our own ways of handling money each generation. Baby boomers grew up with grandparents who lived through the depression and who taught their children—our parents—to be very cautious with money. My parents did their parenting in a world that was strikingly different from the world today.

Besides the variety of current experience, money attitudes change over time. Let's travel back briefly to my preteen years.

It's 1955. I am eight years old, and the United States sets a new record for automobile production with 7,169,108 units. Imported cars number 5,200, or well under one-tenth of one percent of the total. General Motors is the first company ever to gross $1,000,000,000 in a single year. The average weekly take home pay for a family of four reaches $74.04. The most popular consumer magazines cost 20 cents. William Whyte, Jr. writes *The Organizational Man* to describe the rigidity and stuffiness and bureaucratic manner required of male executives. It was a time of obedience to authority and unprecedented prosperity.

Looking back on this period, Warren Bennis says that in the 1950s "America suffered an unprecedented failure of nerve."[27] He comments that after the Kennedys and Martin Luther King were murdered in the 1960s, "the bosses took over again." The 1950s was a decade when a lot of people bit their tongue and did what they were told.

David Halberstam, in his book *The Fifties*, describes Ozzie Nelson, star and writer of the television show *The Adventures of Ozzie and Harriet*, which provided the period's definitive stereotype of American family life. Ozzie Nelson was well qualified to define the classic view of suburban life. He was the nation's youngest Eagle Scout, an honor student, and a former star quarterback at Rutgers. Halberstam comments in his book that while Nelson was a mediocre writer, he was brilliant at creating a portrait of the way Americans *wanted* to look. He showed us without a generation gap, and we liked that illusion.

Let us travel back to 1980. I am thirty-three years old. U.S. automakers estimate their collective losses for the year at $3,000,000,000. That same year there is one divorce for every two marriages in this country. The nation is embarking on a riot of self-indulgence during which the national debt doubles in five years to $2,000,000,000,000 (trillion). Ivan Boesky is fined $100,000,000 for insider trading. The trade deficit jumps to $18,000,000,000. LTV creates the biggest bankruptcy in history with $4,000,000,000 in debt. We discover brie and chardonnay in a big way. Wanton self-indulgence is in fashion.

In 1996, the landmarks are different from anything we have seen before. Standard advice from the past, no matter how good it was, is now obsolete because today's parents were trained differently from their parents, and children face a world unlike any that has come before it.

The variety of stories I encounter in my work justifies a separate book. My appointments with clients are usually structured to allow more than half the allotted time to discovering and listening to their stories. I do this for several reasons. First, it enables me to provide better and more relevant advice. Second, I am convinced it contributes to their emotional and mental health to have an opportunity, a forum, to discuss the sensitive issue of money with a knowledgeable and non-judging professional. Third, it adds to my understanding of what people experience when they endeavor to cope with the issue of money in their lives. Every time I perform therapy on my clients, I also perform therapy on myself. I think that is true for every well-intentioned person who attends to the needs of others.

Teaching money values to children

We can sometimes learn most easily from extreme examples. There is a saying in oil-rich Venezuela: Columbus discovered it. Bolivar liberated it. Oil rotted it. Oil brought in about $8,000 per citizen in the last two decades. In spite of this, four out of ten of them live in poverty. Inflation in 1994 was 71 percent. Money was perceived as endless. "Venezuelans lost their values," says Mary Goodwin, an environmentalist who once worked as a translator for an oil company.

We can use this example to teach us the power of money to

encourage laziness and misconceptions about the nature of wealth.

Children vary in attitudes about money just as adults do, and it is not a simple matter of being taught in a certain way. Teenage Research Unlimited, in Northbrook, Illinois, has discovered that a relatively stable core of about 25 percent of teenagers is "extremely interested in and sophisticated about money."[28] In 1989 a study concluded that teens spent about $56,000,000,000 that year on casual purchases such as food and clothing This is more than double the 1975 figure.

Handling money is important to teenagers both because they handle a lot of it, and because they are developing habits for their adulthood. Some of them will take to it with eagerness and finesse. Others will not. It is important to be clear in your own mind what your values are so that you can compensate for personal biases when you present money handling lessons to your children. Then, it is important to recognize your child's natural bent where money is concerned so that you can meet your child at his or her point of departure.

One of the most important things to develop in young people is a sense of self-esteem where money is concerned. Psychologist and family counselor Kevin Lehman sees the fourth grade as a time when children begin to feel tremendous peer group pressure for the first time. This is the age when a child begins to notice the condition of the family car and the way the parents dress. It is wise to begin to address money issues at this time if you have not already done so in response to your child's questions.

The successful way to do this, in my experience, is to provide the child the opportunity and the encouragement to make informed choices, to notice the results, and to use those results as a guide the next time around. Naturally, "informed choice" has to be tailored to the child's age and circumstances. This approach is in contrast to "discipline" and scolding. Choice A produces this result, choice B produces that result, which way would you like to try, Attila?

Going to the movie today means there will be no possibility of a movie tomorrow, and so on. These informed choices build self-esteem, avoid the creation of destructive feelings of guilt, and build a solid foundation for handling money in a mature way. The effective motivation in life is the response to life itself, not another human beings interpretation of what is "good" or "bad." The sooner a child learns this, the better for his or her willingness to accept responsibility and accountability.

You might propose this: If you get $10.00 per week, and your school lunches cost $1.50 per day, this leaves $2.50 at the end of the week. If a movie and a popcorn cost $5.00 you can afford the treat each two weeks.

In addition to the parental desire for children to prosper and thrive, there are civil pressures to raise responsible offspring. The financial risks parents face increased recently in California. Parents and guardians are now liable for up to $25,000 for willful misconduct by their charges. A change to Section 1714.1 of the Civil Code raised the liability from $10,000. The law is worded carefully to assure the reader that other laws can add penalties too. Children become a part of wholistic taxes in many ways. Liability of this sort is just one of them.

When our children are first born, they are dependent upon us for everything, and as parents we depend on them for validation in many forms. We want our children to do well, not only out of concern for them, but also to reflect well on our parenting skills and as testimony to our dedication and love. Inevitably parents live part of their lives vicariously through their children. It is this temptation to live through our children that often brings unpleasant pressures to bear on them. Overzealousness at little league games is one of the more familiar examples of parents achieving through their children. Unless you have seen this in action, it is difficult to grasp how offensive it can be. We must recognize the unfulfilled dreams that we harbor within ourselves in order to guard against burdening our children with our desire for them to do what we did not do.

John Bradshaw writes, "Letting our children separate is the most important task of parenting."[29] Money is one of the ways some parents keep their children attached to them. As the old refrain says, money isn't everything, but it sure keeps the children in touch.

Having money put away that is destined for the children when the parents die is sometimes a device for assuring that the children will mind their manners and remain attentive. As bizarre as it sounds, parents occasionally use their power to bestow an inheritance as a manipulative device. It happened to one of my clients. His mother gave him an ultimatum. Either do her bidding or be taken out of the will. He opted to lose his inheritance.

Allowances are sometimes used for leverage. Parents may suspend allowances to manipulate their children. I believe this attaches negative connotations to money that create disturbing patterns for the child that are hard to unravel: "If I'm bad, I don't get paid." If they accept this premise at a deep psychological level, it can wreak havoc in adult life. People are pretty thoroughly confused about where money "comes from" in the first place, and to add another layer of moralistic thinking to the money issue is a major disservice to a child. The child becomes an adult who accepts that certain transgressions result in a loss of income. The human mind is sufficiently clever to repeat this experience and to disguise the origins of the problem so that only a professional counselor can identify and "fix" the problem. Why create the problem in the first place?

I recommend separating issues of allowance from issues of discipline. Allowances are to teach money handling skills and to make the purchase of day-to-day incidentals practical and convenient. Keep discipline issues about making the bed and mowing the grass separate. The fulfillment of these responsibilities might be reasonably and properly linked to freedom to go to the movies and go on outings and other forms of recreation. I don't recommend linking them to cash.

Child psychologist Lee Salk warns against creating the impression that money is linked to parental love. When the money supply is turned on and off arbitrarily, or it is indexed to some specific thing a child does, it leads to equating money and love. This is a destructive experience for the child.

The reverse is also true. Money is poorly used as a bribe. I disapprove of bribing children at all, or anyone else, for that matter.

I particularly object to bribing with money. Basically, I recommend the same guidelines for your children that you expect for yourself, only simplified to the level your child can grasp.

It is healthier to give the child space and not burden him to live out our goals for us. The best relationship is supportive without being demanding. We want our children to be successful, but we do them the greatest service when we let them define success their own way. We can assist our children with their college expenses while letting them choose their major. We can help them purchase a home, but let them decorate it without interference from us.

Surviving prosperity

As a certified public accountant, I have many clients who are financially prosperous. They face a particular problem in relation to money and children. The problem is keeping children motivated when they know they're going to inherit a large sum of money. One of the best ways I have seen is to give children money to invest and invite them to spend the earnings instead of the principal. Nobody was born knowing how to invest, and the sooner this education begins, the better. The lessons also require the parent to stay ahead of the child in terms of knowledge and understanding of financial markets. It is a winning situation for all concerned.

It is not uncommon for children to have a fairly sophisticated knowledge of savings and investments at a young age. This can be encouraged by demonstrating that savings are important. A fine example is when parents establish a college fund at the time the child is born. Patrick, who is now five years old, has a fund that many of his relatives have added to on birthdays and at Christmas. It has several thousand dollars in it now, and by the time he is ready for college, he will surely be able to afford the finest institution that will admit him. Let's hope his study habits match his parents' saving habits.

A great way to keep children motivated in regard to saving is to create a matching trust. This trust matches the child's earnings. If the child earns $100, the trust matches it. If the child wants to be a bum on the beach and earn nothing, the trust matches that too. It is difficult for parents who love a child to be strict in this type of arrangement. They let emotions override their desire for the child to succeed. When a child remains dependent in adult life it becomes a question whether parents are doing their family member a favor by keeping him in the will. Would it be better to create an arrangement in which he earns at least a portion of the inheritance? The parents can then coach and instruct instead of taking a passive role. The danger is that the parents will use their position for personal advantage. This happens when they continue to measure their success by the achievements of their children.

Leaving money to the children

I ran into the Howells Friday night, and had the pleasure of telling the little boy a story. He climbed up on my lap and told me he wanted a Bible story. He went to bring the Bible and brought a large dictionary. I told him about Joseph and his bad brothers, and about the fat and the skinny cows. We had a good time; I am longing for the time when I can tell my own boys the stories that children like to hear. I will have to read up a lot of new ones.

—Carl Badger in a letter to his wife Rose, May 13, 1906

I already told the story of my late client who lived meagerly on Social Security even though she had a $10,000 per month income. While few people are this extreme, many are adamant about refusing to spend their principal and live only on interest and dividends. It is important to bear in mind that estate taxes can gobble up as much as 55 percent of an inheritance. I see an increasing number of clients using up their liquid assets and passing on their illiquid assets such as real estate to their heirs.

This works well in that the parent has a comfortable life style and the children are left with an asset that they can sell but which would have been inconvenient or disruptive to sell during the parents' lifetime. The opposite approach is to leave the principal completely intact rather than spending it to maintain or improve the parents' lifestyle. The remaining cash is heavily taxed by Uncle Sam. This is money that probably was already taxed when it was received as income. I see this as a double loss when preserving the cash results in a diminished experience for the parent and it serves mostly to enrich the government.

If you want to bestow larger gifts, you can do such things as paying little Anna's way through medical school. There is no tax on that transaction, Anna will remember you forever, and the money won't go to the federal treasury. If your estate is large, I recommend spending and gifting it down to the $600,000 level that a living trust will enable you to pass on tax free to your heirs, assuming that this expense will produce an increase in your level of joy in life. If you always wanted to do something, this is the best excuse I know of for getting to it! Take a cruise around the world, give away your summer house on the installment plan, or do whatever it may be to reduce your wealth to $600,000 at the end of your life. You can't take it with you, and Uncle Sam knows what he wants to do with it.

A modified version of this plan works for people of more modest means. Let's say Grandma has $100,000 in savings earning 4 percent, and she uses the earnings to pay for vacations. What happens if she is moved by an episode of *Lifestyles of the Rich and Famous*, and now she wants to take a $10,000 trip? Say she spends the money and reduces her $104,000 to $94,000. The next year simple interest brings the total back to $97,760. In time, if Grandma has time, she can skip a vacation or scale a couple of them down, and she returns to her familiar pattern of $4,000 vacations and $100,000 in savings. If she does not have enough time, her heirs can comfort themselves with the knowledge that Grandma got to take her chosen vacation, the one that made her so happy because Robin Leach had the table next to hers in Monaco.

It also makes sense for many people to give cash to would-be heirs before they die. I have a client who has much more money than she requires to live her chosen lifestyle. Poor health limits her ability to travel or pursue other activities. She gives $10,000 per year to her children and grandchildren. This amount is not subject to tax, and she has the pleasure of giving it to them in person. The first rule of estate planning is, "Give, but not until it hurts." Those who apply this advice seem to me to produce the greatest amount of happiness and satisfaction for themselves and for others. They are able to see their heirs enjoy the money. This also provides the opportunity for the elders to teach the recipients practical lessons about money management.

Subsequent gifts can be predicated on responsible handling of initial gifts. This arrangement often provides the key to holding the attention of an otherwise restless young student.

The value of education

The reasons for seeking an education have become muddled. We are no longer sure if we are learning for the love of learning and the salubrious effect it has on our mind, or whether we see it as a method of grooming ourselves for the auction block of employment. The dean of William & Mary's business school recently said that an MBA from that school would increase a student's lifetime earnings by $300,000. Is that the point of education? Even if it is, the arithmetic is questionable. An education from a prestigious college can easily cost $80,000. This amount invested at 6 percent for 40 years would bring in $411,000.

The California government recently demonstrated an increased interest in parent involvement in elementary and secondary school activities. Governor Pete Wilson signed a bill that took effect January 1, 1995, that assures employees they can leave work for 40 hours per year to attend their children's school activities. There are some restrictions. It applies only to companies with 25 or more employees, the sessions can only last 8 hours at a time, and only one day per month is permitted. The employer can require proof that the parent went to school. It is easy to imagine little Annabel writing a note: "Dear Boss: Please excuse Mommy from work today, she is attending my school play."

Chapter Eleven: Money and the Village Elders

Some wag has described what he calls the new [President Woodrow] Wilson dance which runs something like this: "One step forward, two steps backward, hesitate and side step (repeat).

—Joseph Howell in a letter to Preston Richards, April 11, 1916

The village elder probably has to be reinvented. Television, movies, and sports have provided too high a proportion of our role models. The modern equivalent of the tribal Indian chief from folklore must be revised for our times. We need a vision of the village elder for the new millennium. It is up to each of us to contribute to that vision, and to become that elder.

Without such leadership, we fall into many traps of many kinds. Fascination with money does much to twist our world into odd shapes. Hollywood makes the news for its nasty habit of lying to reporters. Baseball owners and players share a mutual antagonism that one writer compares in intensity to racial hatred. Unocal ignores an oil leak for 17 years, and the mess finally wrecks the tiny California town of Avila Beach.

Professional thieves gut the savings and loan industry at taxpayer expense. School officials deal with drugs, a lucrative product to the criminal underworld, with the sadly unimaginative "solution" of welding high school lockers shut and banning book bags. Copping out, concealment of errors, and resorting to clumsy and shortsighted pseudo-solutions have become widespread and highly visible tactics in America.

Money and jobs are concepts that necessarily change over time, and in order to keep pace with those changes, we need to sit down and discuss them. These are topics for long, rambling dialogues in coffee houses or on park benches. Long conversations that aren't headed anywhere in particular provide the opportunity to discover what we know and how we feel about what we know. They provide time to digest what we discover. We can give voice to our thoughts and get our ears' opinion on what is in our head. This practice is common in the business world. They are known as *think tanks.*

This book is being written during a time when American industry has far more production capacity than imagination to keep it busy. We have the ability to make things, but we do not know what to make. The decline in the number of people necessary to work our farms in order to feed the nation has rippled through other industries, too. The things we already make, we have in sufficient quantity for the quality of life we take for granted. Having more of these things would make us all rich, and we consider that to be impossible. It is an interesting Catch-22.

There is an abundance of me-too thinking because for years top management has filtered out innovative ideas and people. The result is that companies began to look more and more alike. Lacking fresh ideas, companies became redundant and lost their customers who merely gravitated toward the biggest vendors for lack of any other selection criteria. The big companies then hire people with the intention of overworking them in order to keep the costs of benefits low. Benefits cost so much per employee, so why not pay overtime until the cost savings disappears? Job candidates are asked openly or tacitly what they are willing to conceal about themselves in order to fit in. The unique mixture of talents and interests they might possess is often deemed a nuisance rather than an asset.

One of the compelling problems today is that people are bored. I submit that a root cause of excessive eating, drinking, and restlessness is boredom. Jobs are often boring. Even if you have the good fortune to love your work, I encourage you to open the Sunday paper in your town and read the help wanted advertisements. Most of the offerings are for cookie-cutter jobs. They emphasize to the applicant that he or she must be a cookie-cutter clone as well.

In 1985 Alvin Toffler wrote of the "novelty ratio" as the share of a company's products that were new at any given time. Novelty springs from employees with originality and imagination and is coming into greater demand as the required novelty ratios increase throughout the world of business. Many companies lag far behind the rapidly advancing frontiers of novelty. The workplace is changing in favor of originality, however, and this is a boon to individuals who know themselves and their talents. The value to society of companies that are open to novelty is that they remain competitive. We have an employment gap because we don't need all of our citizens to produce the things we are accustomed to having. Financial abundance is linked intimately with creativity and receptivity to change.

We can cultivate creativity by making time for it. We need to offer and invite comments on what work is all about. We need to talk to each other. In languid exchanges we can also explore the role of the village elders, those experienced people whose common sense and abiding love of decency and fair play assure that our town is a nurturing place to live. These are the people who own the businesses where our sons and daughters get their first jobs and who see that they transition smoothly from classroom theory to real life. These are the social pillars who support the school system to that it works.

The leaders and role models for these ideals are the village elders. They are those who lead the council meetings, and the ones we seek out privately for advice. They are the ones whose methods and style we use as a point of reference when we strive to define what is right. As we baby boomers age, we become the village elders, ready or not. We must serve as evidence of the value of integrity. We do well to remind ourselves that the word *integrity* means "the quality or state of being complete; wholeness." We need companies that are whole and complete, too.

We need to pay attention to our attitudes about work and money. It is my view that two issues are overdue for examination. The first is that the relationship of money and work has become muddled. People now choose their work in order to get access to money. The second is that for each person, a specific kind of work must be chosen because it contains activities that are natural and meaningful for that individual.

To choose work because it appears to open a path to money brings anguish to the soul, and inevitably results in a feeling of alienation. The alienation is born from ignoring the work proper for each of us. Buddha made a prescription for work on his Eightfold path. He called for "right livelihood" as one of the eight essential components on the path to enlightenment.

Employers usually set the menu of jobs. The burden is on the applicant to prepare to fit into one of the available job classifications. The irony is that when employers cannot invent enough jobs (and this is because employers often avoid hiring imaginative people) the unemployed think they have failed somehow. The system starts to spiral downward as companies layoff the few imaginative people they have, which reduces their ability to adapt, which leads them to more downturns and layoffs.

Thomas Moore, in *Care of the Soul*, speaks of examining an individual's deepest longing to create. This is done by seeking clues to her "opus," her life work. Moore is one of many philosophers who believes that we all have a life work. I find myself in the company of therapist James Hillman and mystic poet Rumi who agree with Moore. It has been my experience that people who are unhappy in their jobs are quick to dismiss the idea that they have a line of work proper for them. They have accepted the premise that work necessarily involves the abandonment of one's inner vision, and that they must choose from what employers offer.

When people discuss these ideas among themselves they clarify and develop a view of their own opus. Reaching for this vision helps define it and energize it. Thomas Moore says all change begins with an <u>exercise of imagination</u>.

Once we know what our talent is we might take a series of positions that each hone an aspect of it. This might seem like a random path to an uninformed observer, but it might make complete sense to the individual when viewed in retrospect. This is a paradigm shift in job training and placement. It puts the individual in the center of the picture, and tailors the job to the gifts and talents of the worker. The Japanese have long believed that a company is a set of people with skills, not a set of tasks. We can learn from that.

Adopt luxury as a way of life

> *We were very, very poor. We have neither milk nor butter; if we want sugar we must make it ourselves and out of beets. We sell our good clothes, that we have brought from Wales to buy flour with. But we are not alone in our poverty. The people are all poor. Brother G. tried to mix sawdust with his bread stuff; but it did not work very well; it made them all ill; still they had to eat what he had mixed up for it was too precious to waste. Oh for a few of the good things we had at home.*

—Ann Williams Davis, September, 1852

My distant relative, Ann Williams Davis, lost her nine-year-old son William while crossing the country in a covered wagon en route to Salt Lake City from Wales. He had fallen asleep under the wagon and was crushed when the oxen pulled ahead. Her account speaks to us of poverty in its most extreme form. It provides me with a point of reference when I counsel people about taxes and retirement plans.

I encourage people to adopt luxury as a way of life. I distinguish between luxury and avarice, however. Luxury is having all you need of the things that matter to you. "Avarice" means "covetousness or insatiable desire." Avarice is wanting what other people have on the grounds that taking it from them creates a sense of power in the person who takes it. Avarice is a trait of bullies.

I know from working with many hundreds of clients that money management, and beyond that, peace of mind, rests on more than techniques. We must navigate among the nastiness of the world, but without losing sight of its innate sweetness. As *Desiderata* so eloquently advises us, "Go placidly amid the noise and haste." It also says, "the world is full of trickery. But let this not blind you to what virtue there is." *Desiderata* speaks rightly: heroism is everywhere, though it seems to be surrounded by skullduggery at times.

The confusion about one's worth in a corporate environment results from the separation of money and work. When we do work that expresses our deep longing, money as an end in itself is less alluring. Those who are obsessed with money are seldom doing the work that nourishes them. A return to the notion that people have proper work, and that it can be recognized by the devotion and love they demonstrate for their work makes clear what we ought to be doing. If we cease to use work simply for its ability to provide access to money we eliminate the temptation to use jobs to get access to other peoples' money.

There have been a number of books written in the last few years about excessive pay to CEOs. In those instances when corporate leaders are misusing their access to the treasury, I believe it is the responsibility of those who can, to protest. Each of us will draw the line defining proper income differently. We do need to take a stand, however.

There may be situations in which the CEO does generate enormous profits that might not have happened otherwise, and it might be appropriate to provide lavish rewards based on achieving or exceeding predetermined goals rather than being granted after the fact at the discretion of the board of directors. Judging the appropriateness of executive pay must be made on a case-by-case basis in a setting in which the shareholders are informed of what is being done.

An increased level of accountability will right the situations in which executives use their privileged position for unfair personal gain. This will happen when our individual bias is for speaking out, not for cowering in hopes of protecting whatever privilege and position we may have at the moment. The notion of the executive suite as a private club will never serve the company or the community.

Destructive demands of unions

Unions were born during adversarial times, and many of them adopted and even improved upon the very tactics they were supposed to defend against.

The litigious mood in America continues to make employers more defensive and less accessible. Legislation being considered as this book is being written would place more responsibility on employers who fire people. This means that unhappy employees can return long after the firing and possibly win large damage suits against the company. This can only exacerbate already strained relationships in the workplace. A new law in California protects former employers who comment to prospective employers about the ex-employees work. The employer cannot be sued for <u>telling the truth</u>. The state of California has officially recognized truth as being appropriate in that situation.

Every year from 1981 through 1990, business eliminated 1,000,000 manufacturing jobs in this country, according to the Bureau of Labor Statistics. Los Angeles County lost 524,000 jobs from 1989 to 1994. An example of the source of these layoffs is Arco, which started its third wave of layoffs in 1994. It was predicted that by 1995, 3,300 jobs, or 13 percent of the work force, would be eliminated from that company. Amoco, another large petroleum company, will release far more.

Middle management also got squeezed in the 1980s, and the 50-50 rule became a modern death rattle: if you are over 50 years old and earn more than $50,000 per year, watch out! Top management began to recognize that middle management was charged primarily with double and triple-checking work that was already done by someone else who knew the task better than the manager. This checking interferes with the flow of information between top management and the front lines. Middle managers became recognized as a hindrance rather than a help, and they were unceremoniously thrown out in droves.

Another major shift in the work environment was top management's move to exploit the companies they ran. In 1980, the average CEO made 42 times as much money as a factory worker. In 1991 this ratio changed to 104 times as much. This is a major shift in priorities that is completely disproportionate with anything in the realm of logic. Executive productivity, if indeed that has anything to do with executive pay, certainly did not double during that decade. In my opinion, America was ripped off by all the executives who took such astronomical pay raises.

Adversarial relationships have handcuffed many American businesses. The cancellation of the 1994 World Series is a vivid example of conflict in action. We need to restore a sense of community within our business organizations. We must think of new ways to build community spirit. The popular press is giving more coverage to this topic. The 65th anniversary issue of *Business Week*, published in October of 1994, devoted the cover to rethinking work and the structure of organizations.

John Handy, author of *The Age of Unreason*, coined the term "portfolio work" to describe a new job profile. The portfolio worker might be a consultant, a part-time employee, a teacher, and an author, with all of these endeavors focused on her specific area of skill and knowledge. This package of activities is intended to replace a traditional "job" in which all services and all pay are exchanged with a single employer as has been the tradition for decades. Entrepreneurship is booming. In 1993, 737,000 corporations were born in this country, and this number does not include sole proprietorships and partnerships.

In this scenario the familiar cycle of promotions and raises tied to time in service is largely lost. Lost also are certainties about pension funds, gold-watches as retirement gifts, and the conspicuous role of others in determining our career tracks. We are on our own to a degree that has not been seen in this country in anyone's memory.

Another revolution in the world of work is that people want it to be satisfying, not sacrificial. Philosophers and saints have affirmed for centuries that people want to work. Work satisfies our deepest longing to create and sustain our world as we imagine it to be. The corporate model is based on the assumption that people work only because they must, and that they work harder in a competitive environment in which their claim to a piece of the pie is tentative at best and always being threatened by someone hungrier than they are.

This rather macabre view has been challenged by the quality experts for decades. As Rafael Aguayo says in his book about Dr. W. Edwards Deming, "Isn't there something obnoxious and silly about the idea that a group performs better when everyone is trying to beat up on everyone else in the group?"[31] Little by little companies are recognizing that competition in its corrosive form reduces effectiveness.

Anger, used as a management tool, also reduces effectiveness, and is contrary to win-win strategy. Team building is on the rise in business. The Japanese developed this concept sooner than Americans, but we are an adaptive people and lessons are not lost on us! Still, some people at the top of the power pyramid use their positions for personal gain. During this transition period during which individual dignity is carried to higher levels of respect, we must still be watchful of how leaders handle our money.

Employers are feeling pressure to make health insurance and pensions to portable so that workers have greater independence. They don't want to find that a corporate raider, drawn by the prospect of plundering an "over-funded" pension fund, has purchased the company in which they have invested 20 years. They don't want to find that the health insurance company has a relationship only with the employer and not with the patient.

The word *integrity* is often taken to mean *honesty*. Integrity literally means the state of being *complete*. When we achieve racial integration in our society, we make our society *complete*. A person of *integrity* has nothing hidden or cast off, no missing parts. The whole person is <u>all there</u>.

This wholeness includes values, emotions, and ideals. It is easy and profitable to deal with a complete person. The more *integrity* we see in leaders and executives, the more confident we can be that whole people are making key decisions in our society. A person of integrity consults his or her head *and* heart when making decisions that affect our jobs, pension funds, and quality of life.

Chapter Twelve: Our Nation as Village Elder

It is not the function of our government to keep the citizen from falling into error, it is the function of the citizen to keep the government from falling into error.
—**Robert H. Jackson, U.S. Supreme Court Justice from 1941-1954**

In our rapidly shrinking world it is essential that our government and our nation remain effective leaders in the global community. Just as we need village elders in our home town, so do the nations of the world need the equivalent. I want to speak out for four steps which I believe are important in order for this to happen.

1. Establish an atmosphere of respect in the election process. A less hostile and corrosive electoral process is necessary to assure that ordinary citizens will continue to participate in government. Elections these days subject candidates to extreme verbal abuse and personal attack. Many well-intentioned people are discouraged from entering politics because it has become so vicious, and we need those people to be active in the political system. We will not have a government of the people if candidates need a prize fighter's capacity for pain in order to run for office.

2. Trim government. We must trim tasks from the government's agenda in spite of the constant demand that the government do more things for more constituencies. The government is neither a baby sitter nor a parent, and cannot be. We must reclaim responsibility at the lowest local level whenever we can. Government is subject to the same laws of efficiency as any other organization. It must learn to be trim and focused.

Effective organizations concentrate on that for which they are uniquely suited. This means that evolving organizations *acquire* new roles and *abandon* old ones. As circumstances change, the evolving organization deliberately yields in those areas where it cannot continue to make a unique contribution, and it recognizes new ways to serve. Alvin Toffler's book *The Adaptive Corporation* explains this concept clearly.

No other organization besides the federal government can properly handle matters of national defense or international diplomacy, for example. However, many organizations can oversee local issues such as providing leisure activities for teenagers and for job training programs. The federal government, like all organizations, must specialize in order to remain vital. Its current state of malaise is due largely to the unwieldy number of tasks it attempts to complete.

Unfortunately, people are demanding more from the federal government, not less. The federal government has become a father figure of sorts in a father-hungry world. The change to slimmer government will begin when the village elders speak up and claim responsibility in our home towns. We have to be an audience that supports politicians who make the tough decisions.

Americans restrain the government's ability to change when they place personal advantage over the public good. Labor Secretary Robert Reich wanted to reorganize 154 federal job-training programs managed by 14 federal agencies into a more efficient and productive system. The General Accounting Office acknowledges that few of the programs are well managed in the $25 billion bureaucracy that handles them.

Administrators don't know if their trainees find work. They don't know if the work they find is the kind they were trained at taxpayer expense to do. The system is a morass of duplication and inefficiency—at the expense of taxpayers and aspiring taxpayers.

Reich wanted to tie things together for greater efficiency. He began with his own department and quickly ran into roadblocks.

According to *Business Week,* "Unions were irate that Reich's plan would undermine the generous $270 million program for workers who lose jobs to foreign competition. Unionized government workers were equally outraged that Reich would let private companies run some one-stop career centers, imperiling bureaucrats' jobs."[34]

It seems that everybody from union leaders to mayors had objections to changes that might take away cash, power, or prestige from them. *Business Week* Reporter Christina Del Valle summarized the situation this way: "Reich thought his 'think small' approach provided the answer to entrenched interests who would resist wholesale change. But he's learning that in Gridlock City, even modest change is to be feared." The restraints on Reich and his efforts arise from a network built of shared values. We, as a nation, don't want our short-term goodies taken from us even in exchange for long-term rewards of greater magnitude. We have a bias for lethargy.

Vice President Al Gore wrote about trimming government waste: "To shut down programs, therefore, we must change the underlying culture of government."[35] The underlying culture of government is based on some basic outdated premises and obsolete ways of reasoning. We cannot, in all probability, change the way bureaucracy works. We will instead have to change from bureaucracy to another kind of government organization. The right kind of organization may not exist yet. The right way to organize government may have to be invented, and to do that, we need to modernize the way we solve problems.

One of the things we must do in order to solve problems is to identify and promote people who know the difference between managing and leading. As Warren Bennis says, managers do things right, while leaders do the right things. Peter Drucker is fond of pointing out that too many managers are good at useless jobs, and they get promoted for their demonstrable skills rather than their appropriateness to the company.

"Times change. The government, mostly doesn't," wrote Tom Peters in the foreword to Vice President Al Gore's book, *Creating a Government That Works Better and Costs Less.* The federal government employs 2,900,000 civilians and maintains a military force of 1,800,000. The manufacturing sector has lost 1,000,000 jobs per year from 1981 through 1990. The federal government, in contrast, keeps growing, though Bill Clinton wants to shrink it 12 percent over a five year period. Employment in government in Washington, D.C. grew five times as fast as the population in general while baby boomers were growing up. This figure does not count the swelled ranks of the lobbyists.

The federal personnel manual is 10,000 pages long. Federal Acquisitions Regulations (how to buy things) fill 6,000 pages. According to one government source, one fourth of all federal employees manage, control, check up on or audit the rest. They consume $35 billion a year in salary and benefits alone.[40]

Complication breeds more complication. Calculating depreciation brings us to a fine example of the complexity bureaucrats can produce. When I was in school there were three basic ways to calculate depreciation: straight line, sum-of-the-years-digits, and declining balance methods. In 1981, Reagan's first tax bill brought us ACRS, Accelerated Cost Recovery System. It had no bearing on any of the previous methods, so tables were created for the calculations. It was designed to benefit corporations, and it was so egregious from the citizen's point of view that even Congress was embarrassed by what it had done and it stepped in to bind some of its more gaping wounds by restricting benefits. One feature that created a stampede was that a company that lost money (and which had no taxes to cut) could sell its excess losses to a profitable company that would then take the losses as a tax deduction from their fat income. IBM bought a $1,000,000,000 in credits from Ford for $100,000,000, or ten cents on the dollar.

Pogo, the cartoon character, announced many years ago, "We have met the enemy, and it is us." Government is us. Government cannot budge from the will of the people as the Reich episode illustrates. Until we develop what Tom Peters calls a bias for *action* instead of our current bias for taking the handout, posturing as power figures, and rejecting change, government will necessarily continue to be expensive, inefficient, and inept. The work begins at home.

3. Think globally. Nothing is truly local anymore. War was once an effective way to increase wealth by plundering your neighbor's treasury. Today it makes no economic sense to attack a country that has McDonald's franchises, and which takes American Express. It's better to do business with them. This is one of the positive changes that has come from thinking globally. Still, there is much to be done.

The tobacco industry is eagerly targeting developing nations as a source of new customers as people in the United States continue to abandon smoking. Can we export this cancer-causing agent to the unwary citizens of other lands and still be credible in our protests about drugs coming in from South America? Are our ethics for sale if the price is right? What are we willing to do for profit?

A headline in the *Orange County Register* for a report on the International Red Cross declared, "Red Cross: Barbarity extensive in world."[31] The Red Cross spent 85 percent of its $579,000,000 aid budget in 1993 in three places: Somalia, the former Yugoslavia, and Rwanda. The remaining 15 percent went to help people in 51 other countries. "One thing is sure," said Cornelio Sommaruga, the President of the International Red Cross, "the chaos and barbarism we are experiencing in the present conflicts is a new phenomenon for us." This statement means that the Red Cross has never seen things get so ugly.

A cruel irony is that this carnage is assisted by weapons built and sold by rich countries like the United States. Sommaruga blames the increase in atrocities on the huge arsenals of weapons stockpiled during the Cold War. Even the poorest countries have them.

The United States has sold weapons to countries whose only moral claim to those weapons was cash to pay for them. This willingness to sell weapons must eventually be traced back to executives whose first priority was profit. It is not possible to separate the profit motive and lack of conscience behind these sales from the whole picture of taxes and responsibility in this country.

Money talks. It is clear that we have influential and powerful people in business in the United States whose greed and avarice are toxic and corrosive. How can politicians, whose fortunes and position depend on our money and votes, be expected to turn this tide of avarice if we cannot do it as citizens, stockholders, and executives?

We must make it clear that we will no longer reward greed with authority and wealth in corporate America. That building process must start at home and spread through our society in waves. As long as lying, deceit, and greed are considered desirable traits for an executive to have, we are not likely to achieve peace in the world.

4. We must replace zero-sum thinking with an organic view of prosperity.

According to the zero-sum concept, a gain for one person necessarily results in a loss for someone else. Zero-sum thinking says the pie is only so big, and your share diminishes my share. It creates an economic model that looks like a pyramid with a small percentage of "rich" people at the top and a whole lot of poor people at the bottom. The zero-sum model is exactly that—a mental representation of one way the world can work. No one knows how many models can be constructed, or how many of them portray systems that work.

What is so convincing about the pyramid model of wealth? Its main claim to fame is that it is the template for the only pattern we have seen succeed on a large scale in recorded history. Pre-historical experience, we assume, consisted of nomadic hunters, none of whom was rich. Each individual was lucky to have an animal skin to wear, a spear, and a cave to live in. What could make such a person rich?

The pyramid paradigm of wealth is no more natural than any other. It is simply the one with which we are most familiar. It can be argued that it is decidedly unnatural, and this becomes more obvious as we as a society become more productive with our tools. It will soon be difficult to justify poverty at all. Sustaining poverty in an increasingly productive world requires more and more ingenious arrangements.

Consider that during fairly recent times, from a historical perspective, kings lacked running water, polio vaccine, television, and countless other amenities that are available to nearly everyone in this country. Now 96 percent of American households have at least one color television. We use these comforts as a baseline and define wealth as how far we rise above it. In 1970 no homes had VCRs. In 1990 there were 67,000,000 of them. Cable television subscribers went from 4,000,000 to 55,000,000 in the same interval.

The pyramid view of wealth requires that we attach value only to that which is rare. If we break that agreement, people who are not supposed to have wealth suddenly have it. Diamonds, for example, are plentiful, and their price is maintained only by virtue of the fact that diamond merchants hold most of the world's supply in reserve off the market. In February 1994, a federal grand jury indicted De Beers Consolidated Mines Limited and business units of General Electric Company on a single count of conspiring to fix prices in the worldwide industrial diamond market. DeBeers dominates 80 percent or more of the $600 million market.

The Justice Department investigated for two years before bringing charges. Is a diamond valuable because it costs a lot, or is it valuable because of its beauty and its usefulness both industrially and as a symbol of marriage? Would more people be rich if they had diamonds, or would people with diamonds suddenly consider them common?

Picasso painted hundreds of pictures that were held out of circulation to keep prices high on those that were in the market. Why are his paintings less valuable when they are numerous? It is because of our acceptance of the pyramid paradigm for wealth. We have tacitly agreed that only so many people can be rich at any one time, and we shape our experience to obey the demands of that paradigm. Keep those diamonds and Picassos hidden away in vaults!

The zero-sum view has a narrow understanding of what "making" money means. It assumes that only so much can "be made." The view has to be consistent with maintaining the pyramid because we have accepted the pyramid model as the final authority, and no contradictions are capable of receiving validation.

We continue to change the meaning of poverty. We must do this to support the fiction that some people have to be poor. Robert Rector, a senior policy analyst in welfare and family issues at the Heritage foundation, a Washington-based public policy research institute, distinguishes between "material" poverty and "behavioral" poverty. His view is that "today's low-income family typically lives better than a middle-income family lived when John F. Kennedy was president."[48] The average new home built in America in 1990 had 2,080 square feet, up from 1,500 square feet 20 years earlier. As an aside, Tokyo and the surrounding area has four million housing units with an average size of about 500 square feet.

Rector explains the increase in the lifestyle of the "poor" in America by pointing out that in 1965, 1.5 percent of the GNP went to subsidize the poor. Now the number is 5 percent. There are 44 major welfare programs in this country, and people frequently receive cash or other support from a number of them at one time. Does a child who gets free lunches at school also get food stamps through his family at home? He can. Seven percent of Americans received food stamps in 1989. The highest concentrations, on a percentage basis, are found in Mississippi, Louisiana, and West Virginia. One person in five received food stamps in Mississippi in 1989.

Contrast that with a member of the armed forces who pays a heavy penalty for eating a single meal in a mess hall that is not paid for in cash if that person also receives a food allowance for living off base. At least that is how it was in the Marine Corps during the Viet Nam war. Welfare recipients have it far easier in that regard than people risking their lives in time of war. The overlap of welfare programs brings 42 percent of recipients to 150 percent of the poverty income. J. Peter Grace states it boldly in his book *Burning Money*: "It means almost half the beneficiaries of poverty programs aren't really poor."[49]

Webster's Dictionary says *poor* means: "Lacking material possessions; having little or no means to support oneself." In practical terms poor means not having access to necessities, specifically because necessities do not exist, or they are too expensive to buy. Statistically, a color television is a necessity, since nearly all poor homes have one. Indoor plumbing graces 99 percent of American homes. It is obvious that the definition of poverty changes with the times.

In order for poverty to occur in a typical modern civilization, with its high degree of productivity, it is required that a high percentage of the population avoid producing things of value. If everyone is usefully employed in a skilled and educated society, poverty becomes difficult to sustain. Busy, well-equipped people produce a lot. The economy brims with things of value. The United States restrains productivity by channeling large segments of its potential work force into prisons, welfare, unemployment, unproductive government jobs, military service, and the underground economy.

Prisons

The U.S. Census reported that in 1990 there were 1,115,111 people in prison. A widely accepted figure used by the Bureau of Prisons says that each prisoner costs $20,000 per year *not including the price of the building or the lost revenue in taxes they would pay if they were working!* When you add those who are on parole and probation, people who do not easily get the kind of jobs where they can produce something, the total exceeds 4,000,000.

The state of California has increased prison expenditures from three percent of the general fund in the mid 1980s to seven percent ten years later. In the next five years the bill for operating prisons will increase another $645,000,000 per year. The state spends $113,000 per cell to build high-security cells. Who likes prisons? The union for prison guards donated $900,000 to Governor Pete Wilson in 1990 for campaign expenses. The *Los Angeles Times* calls the prison building frenzy "A Prison Explosion."

The Clinton crime bill included $7,600,000,000 for recreation centers to hire people to ask youngsters not to join gangs. We used to call crime prevention "good parenting." Now we hire it done, inefficiently, by strangers, at taxpayer expense. House GOP Leader Bob Michel, Republican from Illinois, said of the bill, "there are too many election-year goodies, trinkets and gift-wrapped spending programs piled on it. It now looks like Santa Claus wearing a sheriff's badge."

We do not know how many people a well-structured society puts in jail. We do know that we have the dubious distinction of being #2 in the world with an incarceration rate of 455 per 100,000 people. Only Russia finds more reasons to confine people. Japan, at the other end of the spectrum has a rate of 42 per 100,000 population. We know that 91 percent of California's prisons are over capacity.

Welfare

It is easy to forget that *welfare*, according to *Webster's Unabridged Dictionary*, means "the condition of health, prosperity, and happiness." The government refers to welfare programs as "entitlements." The third meaning of the word *entitle* is "to give a right to demand or receive," as in, working entitles a person to be paid. We are not clear these days on what entitles a person to receive money from the government.

Welfare has a bad reputation in spite of its noble meaning. We have come to think of welfare as minimal support rendered grudgingly to people who take it for granted. The biggest welfare program is Social Security. Most people who receive Social Security paid something into it, but that money was spent long ago. Current retirees are receiving other people's money. Most people agree that it would be a great injustice to take it away from those who are receiving it now. Most will also agree that young people will not receive the benefits. The anguish and the anger come to the surface when we endeavor to draw a line marking the last person to receive the checks.

Welfare puts government in the role of parents and the extended family. We have proven that this approach does not work well. The real cost is to the spirit. People who trade self-esteem for money have lost a great deal in the bargain.

There is a fine old saying, "Give a man a fish, and he eats for a day. Teach him to fish and he eats for the rest of his life." The sentiment expressed in this saying is nourishing to the human spirit, yet we, as a society, have proven ourselves to be poor teachers of fishing. We have opted instead, like divorced absentee parents, to send money to our children rather than taking time to teach them what we know.

Throwing money at a problem seldom works. It costs at least a million dollars in cash to lock a young man in prison for a life sentence. Add to this the various taxes he would otherwise pay into the economy, say $5,000 per year for 40 years, about $200,000 more. It is difficult to examine this scenario and come away convinced that prison is the best approach to most disciplinary problems. One wonders what difference a genuine personal interest in the prisoner might make if it came early in his life. The same is true for people on welfare. This is not to say such a program would be easy to create, but it would be far more nourishing in every way for all concerned, and it would cost less.

A series of articles in the *Los Angeles Times* revealed the cost of crack cocaine addiction. It profiled Sharron Jean Murray whose tragic experience with the drug cost taxpayers an estimated $250,000 in treatment, therapy, punishment, and other costs. The articles quoted many public officials who lamented the amount of money wasted after the worst of the damage was done compared to the relative scarcity of money to prevent problems before they escalate. Indeed, our society must be made whole again if the weak and misguided who fall prey to these chemicals are to be helped before they crash and burn.

The two rules for welfare mothers are to avoid work and to avoid marrying men who work. A sliding scale of benefits that are gradually replaced by earnings would dramatically change the incentives that operate for people dependent on welfare. Public aid was provided to six percent of the United States population in 1989. This translates to 1,517,000 people.

Unemployment

In January 1994 there were 8,700,000 unemployed people in

the United States, and the 1990 census found another 5,200,000 who identified themselves as part-time workers who wanted full-time jobs. If you divide the part-timer's numbers by two (for the shortfall in their schedules) and add them to the officially unemployed, the total is 11,300,000 souls. That is roughly the number of people in management positions across America. It is more than all this country's school teachers, sales people, and secretaries combined. But we are not finished counting yet. The government does not count all the people who are out of work when it tallies unemployed people.

There is a category known in government parlance as "discouraged workers." These are people who have stopped looking for work the previous year. Economist Walter Williams estimates that nearly 5,000,000 discouraged workers have vanished from the unemployment rolls. The real unemployment rate is more likely around 10 percent.[50] One wonders how much these folks, all of them, might produce if they had a job they identified with and knew how to perform. Or, as children ask, "How much wood would a woodchuck chuck if a woodchuck could chuck wood?"

Economists refer to what they call the natural rate of unemployment. This rate, pegged at six percent, is believed to be a threshold. If too many of those people find work, according to conventional wisdom, wages and prices go up. It seems that unemployed people provide leverage for keeping wages where they are. Is it too great a stretch to say that unemployment is an investment that business makes for the purpose of enhancing its bargaining position with employees?

Karen Pennar, senior writer at *Business Week*, projected that unemployment could reach 4.5 percent before triggering wage increases. She speculated that the Federal Reserve Board "may well prevent it from happening—by pushing interest rates up and killing off growth." She concluded, "that would be a tragedy."[51] Within weeks the Fed raised interest three-quarters of a percent.

The unemployed received $23,300,000,000 in 1991 in unemployment compensation benefits. They may have received additional support from other sources. In an effort to recoup expenses, the federal government charges income tax on unemployment payments.

Unproductive government jobs

Al Gore puts the number of make-work federal supervisors at nearly 700,000. He says they consume a payroll and benefits package of $35,000,000,000 per year. I would put the number higher since I consider most of the IRS staff to be necessary only because of the insane complexity of the tax code.

Consider the post office's awkward condition. Congressional investigators from the GAO called it in a two-volume report a "dysfunctional organization." They found 52,000 unresolved grievances in 1993.[52] According to the report, management prefers discipline over all other forms of motivation. How productive is an organization in which managers cannot resolve grievances, and perhaps don't see any need to do so?

Military expenses

A strong military force, and we have about 1,729,000 people in uniform, is essential to our country, but it has been abused by those with the authority to buy extravagant numbers of weapons that now lie rusting and dangerous. In unlikely places such as the genteel countryside around Temecula in Southern California, canister after canister of napalm sits awaiting some solution to the problem of its existence. Only recently did the military admit the press to this storage depot. From the end of the Viet Nam war until 1994 they concealed the magnitude of their mistake. This happens time after time. A nuclear warhead does not enhance anyone's style of living except for a few executives at the companies that produced them at taxpayer expense.

The United States has 14,900 nuclear bombs, according to an estimate published in the *Los Angeles Times*. Thousands of people are on the government payroll to deal with the problems of nuclear waste and the storage of bombs. A plant near the Texas town of Amarillo stores 6,000 bowling-ball size pits of highly toxic plutonium retrieved when some of the 70,000 bombs this nation has built and paid for were dismantled. Who ordered the last few thousand bombs?

This country spends about 8 percent of its GNP on military expenditures. Japan spends one percent or less. France spends between four and five percent. About $7,000,000,000 per year is spent in the nation's atom bomb laboratories.

> **Premise #8 of Wholistic Taxes:**
> **Any inquiry into the way things are,**
> **changes the way things are.**

The national debt

The national debt puts our ability to continue to lead the world in jeopardy. I am concerned that the government does not have the self-restraint to stop spending more than it takes in. We now have a national debt that is self-propelled. It doesn't need anything from us in order to continue growing. In 1994 the national debt was approximately $4 trillion. This amount is so enormous as to be meaningless in terms of everyday reckoning. It is easier to grasp our individual share of this debt, which currently amounts to about $16,000 per person. If you are married with two children, your household total is $64,000, and growing. What happens when the national debt hits $6,000,000,000,000 (trillion) (and it will if the federal budget is not balanced and balanced soon)? The household total debt jumps to $24,000 per person or $96,000 for a family of four. At $8 trillion it works out to $32,000 per individual and $128,000 for the family, about the equivalent of buying a home.

Sooner or later it will reach the point where 100 percent of all dollars raised from income taxes, penalties, interest, sin taxes, gas taxes, all sources, will *not* be enough to pay the interest on the national debt. There will not be enough money left even to pay the congressmen's salaries. This is the main reason I'm concerned about the future of this country. I am an eternal optimist. I have faith in the ability of Americans to work and survive. But the direction Congress is leading our country will inevitably lead us to ruin.

The government tries to balance the budget, but there are many hands out looking for cash. The California wine industry got $5,300,000 in calendar 1994 to support the efforts of 89 wineries to export more wine. The Market Promotion Program pays agriculture $90,000,000 in total.

Wine industry giants Gallo and Seagram bagged the biggest chunks of cash with Gallo getting $2,550,000 and Seagram $385,000. Stimson Lane, a conglomerate owned by U.S. Tobacco, received $10,000. Tiny, elite Silverado winery, owned by Walt Disney's widow, received $4,000.[32] The definition of the word *squander* is to dissipate by scattering. The government does a lot of that.

Senator Dale Bumpers, an Arkansas Democrat, is a staunch opponent of the program. He said, "when you give Gallo Wine $2 million or $4 million, do you know what you get back? Nothing. You have just contributed $2 million to Gallo Wine. That is what you have done." The promotion won by a 62-38 margin and was funded above the Clinton Administration's request of $75,000,000, but below last year's $100,000,000.[33]

Many books have been written about the national debt, and there is little to be gained by going into detail here. I simply want to say that the problem concerns me deeply, and that it is a profound threat to the economic well-being of our children in years to come.

Chapter Thirteen: Other Peoples' Money

A billion dollars here, a billion dollars there, pretty soon it adds up to real money.

—**Congressman's lament, by Senator Everett Dirksen**

I would like to see all members of Congress be required to file their own taxes. This exercise would have to be done under supervision, much like finals for a college course. The results would be examined and grades posted. This simple device would result in genuine tax simplification. All the idle talk and empty promises would end. The people would be served.

Inscribed over the door to the entrance of the IRS office in Washington, DC, are these words of Oliver Wendell Holmes. "Taxes are what we pay for a civilized society." Oliver Holmes, you may recall, was appointed to the United States Supreme Court in 1902 after teaching at Harvard Law School. Many of Holmes's pronouncements on such subjects as free speech are regarded as legal landmarks. He spoke vigorously and eloquently and won a reputation as "The Great Dissenter."

Holmes spoke those words *before* the income tax was created. If he were to see what poor value the government now provides citizens in exchange for their tax dollars, he might want to amend his statement. He might begin the sentence with the word "appropriate." Income taxes take money from individuals, who watch it carefully, to the public treasury, where it may or may not be handled with appropriate care.

Public money has a mystique. Who can catch the sleight of hand as a billion dollars is divided up among many departments and projects? Will anybody miss a few hundred thousand for a special assignment? Pork barrel projects are bad in good times, and devastating during a bad economy. Let us be aware of how tempting big pools of money can be and how frail our value systems are when we operate out of view.

We haven't always had income taxes. On October 3, 1913 President Woodrow Wilson signed the 16th amendment, a law that resurrected the income tax. There had been none since the Civil War. An attempt to restore the income tax in 1893 was ruled unconstitutional, and it took twenty years to get an amendment passed to make it legal. With an average taxpayer in the one percent bracket, and a maximum of six percent, it seemed innocent enough. Many people earned little enough to avoid the tax altogether. Within ten years the maximum rate had been raised to 77 percent.

The information the government wanted from each taxpayer fit on a single page, and the tax law filled 17 pages. Today the familiar two-page 1040 form is supplemented directly by a maze of 33 additional forms and schedules, and the tax law exceeds 3,000 pages. It is not surprising that more than half the 207,423,469 returns filed in 1993 were completed by professionals. More than 46 percent of individuals use professionals.

The tax code, has been "simplified" many times. You can judge for yourself how well this has been done. I attend tax seminars in the fall of each year to be prepared for all the changes in the tax code that I need to be aware of for the following year's filings. I brought home a binder weighing 5 pounds 4 ounces from one of these seminars. It is packed full of changes in the law, and rulings on cases that shed some light on how the IRS interprets its own rules. It isn't getting any simpler as far as I can tell.

Over the years many of the elder statesmen in my line of work have raised loud cries of outrage at each new wave of simplification, and they have used the moment to announce their intentions to slink off into retirement. I'm still too young and have too large a mortgage for wanton displays of rebellion, so each time the tax law gets simpler I hunker down and do my homework.

It is clear to me that the tax code is deliberately made complex and baffling. I suspect this is so that it provides a haven for doing shady deals. Illiteracy used to provide that cover for the ruling powers. After the masses learned to read, and Gutenberg made books relatively affordable by inventing movable type, the power elite needed a new advantage.

Sometimes lawmakers get caught in their own web. In 1986 the tax law was changed to require automobile mileage that was used as a tax deduction to be logged in a special book to be made available for audit. A few months later the wording of the requirement was changed to merely keeping concurrent records. The notes could now be made in an appointment book, for example. The reason was that members of Congress started receiving log books from their accountants. I imagine they turned to them and said, "What's this?" only to be told that they should know, it was in response to their own law. This is one of the rare instances in which the law makers had to lie in the bed they made, and they quickly changed the rules back again.

The reason mortgage interest on two homes is deductible is that so many members of Congress have two homes. It is quite amazing to me that the more you live like a member of Congress, the more pleased you will be with your tax bill.

Raising taxes doesn't help

The more money the government takes in, the more it spends. This is part of the reason that raising taxes does not solve our deficit problem. One other reason that raising taxes seldom works is that the people nearest the lawmaking process can create conditions favorable to themselves, so they don't get taxed like you think they might. Also, oppressive taxes discourage economic activity, with the result that there is less business on which to pay taxes. You can only squeeze the goose a certain amount before the golden eggs become smaller and less frequent.

Rush Limbaugh makes a strong case in *The Limbaugh Letter* about the futility of disproportionate taxes on the rich. "History shows that raising the tax rates *on* the rich does not result in greater tax revenues *from* the rich."[34] Raising tax rates is tied to zero-sum thinking which assumes that there is only so much pie and the object of the game is to grab a bigger piece than the next guy. Lowering taxes gives people room to breathe. It gives them an incentive to build something which will generate even more tax revenues because the generation device is so much more robust and far-reaching.

Taxing corporations is a mixed blessing. On one hand, it brings in money to the treasury. On the other, it raises prices that consumers pay for whatever it is that the corporation produces. As with all dilemmas, there is no single right solution or course of action. Dilemmas call for making the best of difficult situations and remaining alert to the need for balance. Untaxed corporations would quickly be abused by people who would exploit this feature. In my opinion, there are better ways to collect money than punitive taxes on corporations. Use taxes, also known as sales taxes, match the tax burden to the end user of the product but without inflating the manufacturing cost of the product. Changes in the tax code must be constrained by the need to balance the whole system. Efforts to tinker with tax revenues by dipping into corporate profits can be, and often are, counter productive.

Telling politicians what we want

Voting has been described as a blunt instrument, and indeed, it is a simple gesture. Casting a vote conveys almost no information about our views on policy. Voting happens so late in the political process as to be little more than an afterthought. In spite of the write-in option, it is meaningful to vote only for candidates who are on the ballot. Candidates get on the ballot by surviving a passage through a maze in which countless behind-the-scenes forces influence the outcome.

Money, special privilege, and an elaborate system of favors and debts all have a role in determining who runs for office, and more importantly, who gets the support of those who run the parties. The higher the office, the more the political machinery concerns itself with who is successful and who is not.

It is not much better when we vote for measures. Measures often contain elements that we favor and also elements to which we object strenuously. When we vote for measures, we are often confused about whether supporting a position calls for a yes vote or a no vote due to the deliberately confusing wording of the promotional materials that clutter modern campaigns. We may also vote for an issue or a candidate because we want to be supportive, or we may be voting reluctantly as the only way we see to oppose the alternative choices. Voting is important, but it limits us to yes or no answers on complex matters that have nearly been decided already by people who work beyond the sight of the voter.

The informed and uninformed citizen alike have one vote. Mark Twain described in a short story a world in which people with education and property had multiple votes according to their accomplishments. This has not happened in real life, but Americans who want to express themselves beyond the voting booth know that there are many avenues to political change more effective than voting.

Who votes? Studies show that people with more money and education vote more. The meaningful differences in political posture seem to be not between voters and nonvoters, but between economic classes.

Poor people, quite logically, are concerned with issues concerning home, food and jobs—survival concerns of an immediate nature. Rich people are in a position to broaden their concerns to ecology, national policy, and international relations—survival concerns of a more abstract sort.

Not surprisingly, rich people give more money to political campaigns. Political party activists tend to be affluent, educated and opinionated. Liberals, research shows, participate in demonstrations in greater numbers than conservatives. With these minor exceptions, the "silent" people think pretty much like the outspoken people.

It is interesting to note that scholarly research into voting reveals that voters and nonvoters feel pretty much the same about most issues. We could speculate that nonvoters stay away from the polls because they think their votes would be redundant, not because they lack concern about the outcome.

The great equalizer in political influence is that people in all but the poorest economic classes can contribute time and effort if they choose. Unlike voting, there is no limit to the quantity of self-expression that can be achieved through communication. Everyone can express political views by writing letters, making phone calls, working as volunteers for candidates and incumbents, participating in public demonstrations, and working to influence and persuade on the local level through conversations, speeches, and the like.

As participatory citizens, voting becomes one component in a complex pattern of political activism, and it is not the most influential one. The more qualified the candidates, the less important voting becomes. If all the candidates who reach the final ballot are excellent, voting becomes more of a stylistic issue than a matter of dire choice, good or evil, feast or famine. I favor using our individual influence on politics not so much to favor one party over another as to upgrade the whole political climate by showing that we notice and that we care what they do. Our attention will improve the entire electoral process.

We can and ought to involve everyone who works for us in the task of showing government that we are watching and that we care about what is done there. Our trade associations, and those of people who work for us, provide an excellent place to begin this effort.

IRS Commissioner Margaret Richardson said in a speech to a group of accountants, "I find it puzzling that the AICPA membership has not been more vocal, for example, in seeking an expansion of the electronic filing program to accommodate corporate and partnership returns." She was urging her audience, a professional group of CPAs, to demand more of itself and the IRS. I point this out to emphasize that you are not alone in your effort to change government. Everyone who works for you is a potential agent for change, including your CPA.

I think she misinterpreted the lack of enthusiasm on the part of CPAs. Government electronic tax filing programs are flawed, and the number of bogus returns is painfully high. Before they will get more involvement, they need to improve the efficiency and accuracy of the system.

Ms. Richardson announced a busy agenda for change when she made that speech. She was asking for accountants to put their shoulder to the wheel to assist in implementing that change. You can express your interest in progress any time you conduct business. Make full use of the resources that professionals have available to them. Insist that they act on your behalf within the context of their area of expertise. They literally owe you this service. It comes with the fees you pay them for services rendered. If your CPA disagrees, you might want to get a different one.

Politics is boring and distasteful to many people. My guess is this is because campaigns have become increasingly bitter on a personal level over the years. Campaign speeches have less and less of the sort of content that makes a difference to voters. Michael Huffington spent $25,000,000 in his effort to become a U.S. senator for the state of California, and hardly anyone knew his positions on the issues. The newspaper in his own town of Santa Barbara said it didn't know where he stood on the issues. The sum total of electoral information is confusing. The California voter's pamphlet is a case study in unreadability.

Some of us are simply unconcerned about problems on the distant horizon. A Gallup poll in 1947 asked respondents to identify the biggest problem facing their family. That year 6 percent of those interviewed said there was no problem worth mentioning. In 1967 the same answer came from 16 percent. In 1977 the serenity had spread to 21 percent of those queried. In 1977 Gallup learned that 25 percent of Americans thought Jimmy Carter could balance the federal budget during the next four years. Another 18 percent didn't know if he could do it or not. That is 43 percent of Americans who did not see the deficit problem as urgent. It turned out that Carter didn't balance any of his budgets. We have not seen a balanced federal budget since 1969, and even that was the result of bookkeeping wizardry having to do with how social security was shown on the books. As recently as 1977, balancing the budget wasn't a big issue on the minds of citizens. A Gallup poll revealed that the number one problem in 1977 was the high cost of living, the number one concern for 32 percent of Americans. Excessive government spending seemed a problem to only 3 percent of those surveyed.

A survey by the American Council on Education in 1967 revealed that 51 percent of freshmen "thought it was important to keep up with politics." By 1982 the same survey showed that the percentage of freshmen concerned about politics dropped from 51 percent to 38 percent. "More important to the younger ones is finding a way to make ends meet," says demographics expert Cheryl Russell.[35]

The effect, I believe, of losing sight of politics is that our neglect comes back to haunt us in the form of a permissive, bloated, unwieldy government that creates its own agenda rather than doing the will of the people. The government turns inward on itself and gets lost listening to its own feedback.

Voter turnout at midterm (non-presidential) elections, peaked in 1966 at 48.4 percent of voting age citizens. In 1986 and 1990 it slid to 36 percent. In presidential elections the averages run about 15 percent higher. Midterm does not mean unimportant. The 1994 California midterm election included races for 101 of the 120 seats in the state Legislature, all 52 California seats in the U.S. House and seven other state constitutional officials. This is in addition to choosing a governor and a U.S. senator. Add to that the city races. Huntington Beach in 1994 had 22 candidates running for city council.

Voting is often for cynical or sarcastic reasons. People who vote feel entitled to gripe. People vote against worse or worst candidates. A popular bumper sticker proclaimed, "Don't vote. It just encourages the bastards."

When only a third of adults vote it demonstrates to politicians that they need not address all Americans. Like any smart marketer, they concern themselves with the opinions of those in the audience who are likely to take action. The two-thirds who will not budge from their couches need not be considered; they are irrelevant. At minimum, we need to raise voter turnout just to show that we are not asleep. Even if a citizen votes on only one issue, or one candidate and ignores the rest, it shows that democracy is alive.

In the 1800s voter turnout exceeded 80 percent. Germany's elections in 1994 drew 85 percent of adults to the polls. It is possible to engage the citizenry in voting. Voting in the 1990s is admittedly not fun. Radio and television personalities openly acknowledge the corrosive nature of political rhetoric and the unlikeliness of getting honest information about the candidates. Michael Huffington spent $3,000,000 of at least $25,000,000 campaign expense on spin doctors who advised him, apparently, to conceal rather than proclaim his principles and objectives. The *Santa Barbara News-Press* published a story headlined "Handlers keeping Huffington's image out of focus." It was the most expensive senatorial campaign in U.S. history. The Associated Press called the Huffington/Feinstein competition "notably nasty and personal."

Surprisingly awful

The California voter's pamphlet is challenging reading, even for a skilled reader with the patience to analyze the deliberate deceptions, rampant hyperbole, and contorted legal language that characterize the publication. Advanced reading skills are typical of the minority of citizens, not the majority, so for most people, the voter's pamphlet adds little light to the complexities of voting. California is not unique in this regard. Missouri passed a law that seems to defy interpretation. Some people think it is intended to outlaw gay sex. Others say it is against sex without consent. Attorney Dan Viets wrote about the measure in the Missouri Association of Criminal Defense Lawyers newsletter, fall of 1994. He said the measure "appears to outlaw any purposeful sexual contact." An analyst at the University of Missouri commented, "I know a lot of legal writing is not very clear, but this seemed surprisingly awful, even for legislators."

The most significant new development in voter education may be the emergence of computer on-line services. California devised a system to provide nearly instant voting results from the 1994 election over the Internet system. A professor at UCLA helped design the system which will give computer users voting results faster than they can obtain them through traditional sources such as television broadcasts.

The World Wide Web and electronic mail have ushered in a whole new day in terms of communicating with our elected officials. Check out *Yahoo* and look through the Government Indexes list. A site called *Election Activist* provides instant e-mail links to state and federal officials. A site called *Zipper* will tell you, based on your five-digit zip code, who your elected representatives are. Yahoo's address is http:/www.yahoo.com.

Never has it been so easy to speak out to those who govern!

Who needs politicians?

Do we need elected officials anymore? John Naisbitt, author of several famous books including *Global Paradox*, argues that political parties are dead, but leaders haven't noticed yet. Elected officials were important when there was an information float. Now we can be privy, via television, to news while it happens. All we really need is a response mechanism. We could vote several times a day electronically. As Naisbitt points out, we have the same information and knowledge as politicians. We are on the scene just as they are. We can be sure to attend to votes we consider critical. The voting records of our elected officials reveal that they do not always value the opportunity to vote as consistently as we might like. Why do we need them to express our priorities? We can make our own judgments and get them off the tenterhooks that keep them immobilized as they try to avoid offending a diverse constituency.

Nearly everyone has something useful to say and some contribution of time or talent that would make a difference socially and politically in this country. Action must occur locally because a distant bureaucracy cannot possibly be effective dealing with situations that are subtle or complex.

We would make our government more effective if we laid out to our elected officials our intentions to assist them. We might say: I think "x" would improve this country, and you can count on me to perform "y" and "z" in order to make it happen. Take that promise, Mr. Legislator, and do something productive with it.

Government is ineffective because we shove elected officials into a bureaucracy (the least efficient form of organization ever invented), make them sitting ducks for lobbyists who have money and influence, and then put their feet to the fire to please an argumentative, judgmental and highly fragmented constituency. Then we blame them for failing. Let the citizen who is without sin cast the first stone.

Better yet, instead of casting stones, let's cast a new government. Let's change the process that creates so many errors to a process that creates fewer errors. Again, the resistance to change comes from people who feel threatened by the proposed changes. Technology will soon make it simple for virtually all of us to vote daily, if need be. Senators and representatives could still debate the merits of issues, but they would not have authority over them. We would have the authority, and we would express our decisions by voting electronically. The only problem is assuring that people only vote once. Surely this safeguard is achievable. The method that comes quickly to mind is one's Social Security number plus a four-digit number like ATM cards use.

We can watch congressional proceedings on television. We can know as much of the legitimate information about issues as Bob Dole or Al Gore know. The only thing we don't know is the behind-the-scenes deals, fears and manipulations that paralyze and pollute the job of governing this country.

Voting is boring. The elective process is abrasive and rude. Voter's pamphlets are all but unintelligible and are filled with hyperbole and efforts to disguise the truth. The choice of candidates is usually disappointing, and the campaigns are typically ugly in tone and content.

We need to restore the joy of voting by bringing the process into step with modern times. Let's get democratic again in the classical sense of the word. "Demos" is from the Greek word meaning "people." "Kratein" means to rule; together they provide the basis of our word democracy. When The People are not voting, they are not ruling. When The People are not ruling, the way opens for other forms of government contrary to democracy to operate in plain sight. The word for government by a small, exclusive class of people is "oligarchy." Lobbyists, and the people who fund them, constitute an oligarchy. This group is exclusive by virtue of its wealth. Only those powerful in money can participate.

Rule by the rich, called "plutocracy" is not possible in an active democracy, but it can solidify right before our eyes if we are a sufficiently apathetic electorate. The oligarchy is free to influence with money since elected officials know that money, not a broad base of concern on the part of citizens, drives the machine called politics. The only way to restore democracy is by voting—widespread, chronic voting. When bumper stickers admonish us to "Vote early and often" it will be a sign that the responsibility of participating in government has reached the consciousness of the people.

The remedies that I propose for these problems are as follows.

First remedy: All things change when examined

Premise #8 of *Wholistic Taxes* states that any inquiry into the way things are, changes the way things are. Physics, the branch of science that studies matter, has learned that we cannot examine the physical world without changing it. This is simple to grasp when you consider that studying anything involves interfering with it in some way. It might be by shining light on it, getting near it, making it stop moving, or intervening in any of dozens of other ways. The pursuit of knowledge changes the world in this direct manner.

On the metaphysical level, Deepak Chopra says that knowing the right attitude is sufficient. By this he means that the simple act of acknowledging truth starts things moving. Somehow, truth does something on its own without additional visible effort from us. He was speaking specifically of creating affluence when he offered this advice. It is consistent with biblical advice which frequently includes the word faith. When something seems so real to us that we move to align with it, we can say that we have faith in that idea.

This is to say that awareness, in and of itself, sets power in motion. Attention from outsiders breaks up the clubby, self-serving culture within an organization without any confrontation at all. The awareness and display of interest as such, makes a difference to people and helps keep them honest.

Second remedy: Show respect and earn respect

The ugliness of political campaigns is a symptom of our lack of leadership. Candidates no longer have "esteemed opponents." Instead, the opposing candidate is portrayed as a moral disaster, a liar and cheat. This contempt for the opposition is divisive and corrosive. Restoring dignity and respect to the political arena can only start in small ways, and the chief obstacle to it is that we have made our society brittle and fragile. People who take initiative are bound to offend somebody.

Businesses could reward voters in a way appropriate to each business. Voting stubs could be used to enter drawings for an extra, paid day off, or other prizes. Business owners are village elders. It is up to them to demonstrate at the most basic level that we care about citizenship and responsibility.

A readable version of the voters' pamphlet would make a positive difference. Schools could make rewrites of sections of the voters' pamphlet part of the curriculum. It would educate the students on the issues while it taught them how to eliminate obfuscation and raging hyperbole. Few people read the manuals that are packed with computer software because they are so poorly written. Most of us buy third-party instruction manuals. Why wouldn't we buy a readable version of the voters' pamphlet? In order to attract an entrepreneur to this task, we would need to demonstrate some interest in the subject of voting!

Changes in technology are quickly opening doors to a host of new ways to make ourselves heard. Politicians are faced with the need to reinvent their jobs. We need them, but we don't need them in the old, familiar ways. The next few years will be exciting times in which the power of the individual expands in ways that have never been possible!

In Closing

Absence of respect, courtesy, manners, or admiration creates a state of poverty irrespective of the amount of money you have in the bank.

—Deepak Chopra, Creating Affluence

This book is necessarily leisurely and contemplative because it seeks to trace the influence of money from the privacy of our individual purses to the halls of government. It asks a patient reading.

An appreciative examination of our past makes our haste seem less natural. When we learn our history, we get some relief from the urgency of the moment. We become aware that our life operates in cycles, much like the eternal pattern of the seasons. We sense a naturalness in letting investments *mature*. We develop a deeper appreciation of *balancing* the books.

In order to contemplate our past we must capture it in some way. I am fortunate to have five volumes of writing and photographs that provide a history of the many people who preceded me in the Maughan family. I encourage you begin to capture enough of the texture of your life to convey the richness and dignity of it to those who will follow you, if you are not already doing so.

This will provide a foundation for those that follow to build their own awareness of their place in family and community. Out of this springs patience and respect for all things. Much of the pain of our times is based on peevishness. *Peevish* means "apt to mutter and complain, quick to be annoyed." The baseball strike of 1994 was a symbol of our national peevishness. Neither side found real peace in spite of the enormous amounts of money and adulation they receive as rewards for playing a game. In spite of their privileges and income, they are displeased, they don't have enough. The quarrel appears to be between players and owners. Somehow the fans, who bankroll the sport, are irrelevant.

Peevishness is not the result of a flaw in people. It is a *condition* that reflects a vacuum in leadership. The level of anger in this country is high. In any group of people, anger develops when there is not enough nurturing discipline. I believe that is the pivotal issue of our day. We are hungry for a nurturing discipline, and each of us can be a source of that discipline. After all, the word means "to prepare by instruction."

Our corporations and factories can now produce everything we need with a relatively small percentage of the population working. Our industry, the way it sees itself now, simply doesn't need everyone. We don't know what else to make or where to find new customers. This scenario calls for imagination.

Wholistic taxes, as a concept, will continue to change in many respects. This is because our environment changes, and money management is necessarily tied to the environment. Advice about money must be fresh in order to be relevant. Two fundamental concepts remain the same, however, regardless of what news items fill the daily headlines. These are: everything is interconnected, and win-win works best.

The premises of Wholistic Taxes expand on these two basic ideas, but they just add detail. They affirm that personal choices are important to society and that examining a thing changes it. They affirm common sense: write down your plans, spend money to gain rather than to avoid, and recognize when you can make a difference and when you cannot.

The real essence of Wholistic Taxes is to remain true to simple basics of the Golden Rule and trust your common sense. Everything else is just embellishment on those two themes.

We can now invent a new vision of tomorrow. I am confident that we can, and I am excited about doing it. It is a task for the imagination, for working together, for community effort. It is a wonderful task! It is the task for our times.

Appendixes

Appendix A— Glossary

Avarice

Avarice is insatiable desire, especially for things that belong to another. It is desire that is unhooked from need, usefulness and joy. Avarice involves coveting in the negative sense of that word. (The primary meaning of the word covet is constructive and positive. It means to desire eagerly.)

Baseline

As used by therapist and money counselor Olivia Mellan in her book *Money Harmony*, it is the set of values about money that you take for granted. This set of values consists of your basic nature and temperament *plus* any conditioning by family and environment that have added to this base.

Many of these additions can be neutralized and disassembled once they are identified and found to be needless complications. This returns the individual to his or her native baseline which generally results in greater harmony with money.

Broke

Broke is the past tense of the verb break. The first definition of break is "to cause to part or divide by force." It also means "to disengage." Being broke in the financial sense means the same thing. We are separated from the community of exchange by an act of violence. It is a result of withdrawing in some way that is against the natural order. Our natural condition is to have money. Our word for the physical symbol of wealth, the paper and coins themselves, is "currency." The word currency means "a flowing, running, or passing." Being broke is the condition of interrupting the current, or breaking it off.

Bureaucracy

A form of organization consisting of compartments governed by an inflexible routine and subject to highly concentrated authority in a hierarchical structure. Bureaucracies are designed to be inflexible and to stretch communication lines ever thinner as the organization grows. Communication bottlenecks are inevitable. Bureaucracies are a flawed design due to the fact that they are unwieldy when they get large and they have no mechanism for limiting their growth. The United States government is an example of a bureaucracy.

Comfort zone

One's comfort zone is that area immediately surrounding one's baseline. For some people this zone is quite narrow, and even tiny deviations are upsetting to them. Others can roll with the punches and use variety of experience as a positive learning tool.

Conserve

The primary meaning of the word is *to keep in a safe or sound state.* Resistance to change is properly in the interests of preserving safety.

Currency

Literally, a flowing, running, or passing; a continued or uninterrupted course like that of a stream. Also, that which is passed from hand to hand, that which circulates.

Discipline

The dictionary definition is "training that develops self-control." We can learn discipline in financial matters both as individuals and as citizens.

Discouraged workers

In order to keep unemployment figures as low as possible, the government deducts the long-term unemployed from the rolls of the freshly unemployed. These people are referred to as discouraged workers the year after they lose their jobs. The government also assumes that new businesses create jobs at a rate that cannot be proven. This makes their assessment of unemployment immune to challenge.

Dots (solution to puzzle on page 43)

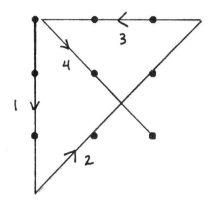

Economics

The dictionary calls it "the science that deals with the production, distribution, and consumption of wealth." I am not an economist. It seems to me from my vantage point that the science of economics is due for the same sort of revision that has come over the physical sciences in the last century. Physical science followed Newton's thinking for years and created a model of the world that resembled a clock. If you knew enough about the gears, you could predict all the motions of the clock. Now science recognizes that the observer participates in creating that which is observed. I am confident that this is equally true of economics, but the prevailing economic scientists are well behind in the advances in physical science, especially quantum physics.

Economy

Economy is derived from the Greek oikos, a word relating to "house" in the broadest sense of the meaning. Economy means "careful management, avoidance of waste." We might define "careful" as the practice of making informed choices in order to preserve and protect something of value.

Federal Deficit	Total	10 Year Increase
(Billions)		
1973 $14.8	431.4	132.1
1983 207.8	1,377.2	945.8
1993 286.6	4,351.2	2,974.0

In the decade from 1983 to 1993 the deficit tripled. Interest paid each year in 1991, 1992, and 1993 was more than the total debt in 1960.

Golden Rule

In the King James translation of the Bible, Matthew 7:12 reads: Therefore all things whatsoever ye would that men should do to you, do ye even so to them. We more often hear it, do unto others and you would have them do unto you. It is the best advice I have found on how to live. It is simple, and to the extent that I have mastered it, it has produced excellent results for me.

Greed

Greed is the act of resisting or avoiding something by obsessively pursuing its opposite. The reason greed produces so little satisfaction is that the goal is not to achieve a positive outcome, but rather to continue to flee from something that is deemed frightening or repulsive. If poverty is sufficiently frightening, a person may pursue money endlessly, thinking that money provides a barrier to poverty.

Holism

According to *Webster's*: "The view that an organic or integrated whole has a reality independent of and greater than the sum of its parts."

Independently wealthy (in a financial position to retire)

Independently wealthy means to me that no effort is required of the individual to provide for his or her financial needs beyond that which is already in place. This person can work or not work without the need for money influencing the decision. The biggest single variable for most people is the presence or absence of a mortgage. Retiring mortgages makes it much easier for people to become independently wealthy.

Junk debt

A credit purchase for something that immediately loses its cash value is junk debt. Examples are clothes, restaurant meals, travel, and the like. Credit cards are properly used by paying the balance due when the bill arrives and for purchases that retain their value, at least over the life of the debt.

Learning loops

Single-loop learning

This is an examination and treatment of behaviors without identifying the underlying causes of the behaviors. It is like giving aspirin for a hangover without addressing the patient's drinking problem. It is like resolving a fight over a seat on a bus without recognizing that a deep-seated racial antagonism exists between the two combatants. (See double-loop learning.)

Double-loop learning

This is learning that looks past the surface to the underlying beliefs that prompt us to do what we do in the first place. It requires venturing past whatever layers of denial and cover-up operate within the organization being investigated. Double-loop learning asks "What are the real causes?" rather than, "Can we eliminate the symptoms?" (See single-loop learning).

Limited partnerships

Limited partnerships are those that have one or more general partners and one or more limited partners. They were named such because the limited partner's liability is no more than the initial investment. Other personal assets of the limited partner are not liable to be attached if the partnership goes bankrupt.

Limited partnerships have cost major brokerage houses hundreds of millions of dollars in recent years either as the result of lawsuits by disgruntled clients or as an act of apology to clients who were mislead and otherwise abused.

Luxury

According to the not-very-revealing dictionary definition, luxury is anything that is beyond that which is essential to life or which exceeds reasonable boundaries.

Dr. Deepak Chopra, with whom I agree on this point, recommends adopting luxury as a lifestyle. I suggest that we define luxury as having enough of everything that matters.

Meso-economics

The prefix 'meso' means in the middle, intermediate. A meso-economic view recognizes the function and importance of industries as the middle ground between the individual and the total national economy. The United States deals primarily with individuals and the country as a whole. Industries are encouraged to trick, trap, gobble, and deceive one another in a macabre interpretation of Darwinian survival contests.

In Japan, meso-economics is the norm. Industries cooperate for the purpose of expanding the total market.

Opus

A work or composition.

Other peoples' money

I include this word in the glossary to invite a moment of contemplation about what it means to you. Congress spends other peoples' money all the time.

The word ecology is derived from a Greek work that means "house" in the broadest sense of the word. Our lives take place on our home planet, and ecology is the study of how to live here unobtrusively and appropriately. The planet's resources seem, to our limited vision, to be up for grabs, to have no owner. Many with this view plunder freely on the assumption that they can act without unpleasant consequences to themselves.

This ecological view of the planet can be narrowed to the level of public responsibility in government. When resources seem to have no owner, we might trace the connecting threads, however slender they might seem to us, to see where they lead. Just as fresh air and rain forests are connected to all of life on Earth, so are public financial resources connected to all who contributed them.

Paradigm

A pattern, example or model.

Political leanings

Left

As a political term, left means "favoring reform or progress." It denotes a resistance to structure and authority, and assumes a bias in favor of spontaneous changes that favor individual self-expression over the rigidity of law. The left wants laws changed to suit the mood of the people. The left is biased toward the leveling of privilege across society. The leftist point of view, carried to an extreme, produces socialism and communism. (Also see Right.)

Right

In politics, the right favors structure and continuity over adaptability. The right wants people to accept and adapt to the prevailing laws. The right is more Darwinian, in contrast to the left, and applauds achievers and survivors who prevail over obstacles. It holds that strict and demanding rules strengthen society as a whole, and it is more sympathetic to public order than to individual needs.

The right point of view, carried to an extreme, produces dictatorships that preserve rules at any and all cost to the individual. George Orwell's book *1984*, in spite of its dated title, is an informative literary portrait of a society that moved too far to the right. (Also see Left.)

Premises

These are the premises of wholistic taxes.

#1 All personal choices are significant to society.

#2 Prosperity is a measure of how our relationships are working.

#3 You can only change behaviors at decision points.

#4 Learning to work *ad hoc* is essential to a coherent society.

#5 Money is more than numbers on a page.

#6 Spend to build net worth, not to reduce taxes.

#7 Intentions produce greater results when committed to writing.

#8 Any inquiry into the way things are, changes the way things are.

Prosperity levels

Poor

Webster's Dictionary says 'poor' means: "Lacking material possessions; having little or no means to support oneself." In practical terms poor means not having access to food, shelter, clothing, and safety, specifically because they do not exist, or they are too expensive to buy.

In order for poverty to occur in a typical modern civilization, with its high degree of productivity, it is required that a high percentage of the population avoid producing things of value. If everyone is usefully employed, poverty becomes difficult to sustain because the economy brims with things of value. The United States restrains productivity by channeling large segments of its potential work force into prisons, welfare, unemployment, unproductive government jobs, and military service.

Rich

I define rich as having enough money to do all your favorite things as often as you want to the extent that money is the determining factor. Naturally, you will be limited in some ways by other considerations such as time, health, social custom and law.

Metaphysically speaking, being rich is having enough of those things that make you feel you are living out your unique and genuine personal experience. All of us operate at some percentage of that ideal. Most of us are confused about what that ideal is for us as individuals, and we chase rainbows that are created by advertising and by peer pressure. John Bradshaw explains that when we attempt to please others instead of expressing our own nature, we lose sight of what is real for us. (See his *Creating Love.*)

The government definition of rich is highly subjective and seems to change with the needs of the moment. Promises to "increase taxes only on the rich" may or may not mean you!

Responsibility

The underlying meaning of responsibility is the "ability to respond." Responsibility "requires an answer" according to the dictionary definition. It is an abuse of the word to say that terrorists were responsible for a bombing, for example, especially when they immediately go into hiding. The proper word for terrorists is "blame." They accept blame, not responsibility. Responsibility, in the full sense of the word, includes the ability and willingness to explain, and if necessary, to make amends. Responsibility is always a virtue, and to the degree that one lacks virtue, one lacks responsibility.

Retire

According to Webster's: "to withdraw; to draw back; to go away to a private, sheltered, or secluded place; to retreat from danger, action, or battle."

Serendipity

The word means "an aptitude for making pleasant discoveries by accident." It was coined by Horace Walpole, a prolific English writer and historian born in 1717. If you drilled for water and found oil, you might term that serendipity, provided you weren't dying of thirst!

Synchronicity

Synchronicity is the interrelatedness (real or imagined) of two or more events that have no apparent causal connection between them. Once, when I was a reckless young man, I picked up a hitch-hiker on the way to a party, and invited him along to the gathering. He met a woman there whom he later married. I think that was an example of synchronicity.

Squander

Squander means to dissipate by scattering. This is one of the common methods of handling money. It is useful to identify what money, in the abstract sense, "feels like" and what the acts of spending and saving feel like. The comparisons are necessarily quite metaphorical. Metaphors provide basic insights into values and beliefs.

Tax

Webster's says: "A compulsory payment of a percentage of income, property value, sales price, etc. for the support of a government." Secondary meaning relates to putting a heavy burden on someone or something.

Tinkering

Tinkering is W. Edwards Deming's term for making changes that manipulate or disguise symptoms instead of identifying root causes and making systemic changes to eliminate symptoms entirely. Organizational scholars refer to tinkering as 'single-loop' learning. Learning that transcends the visible problem to identify and remedy its underlying cause is called 'double-loop learning.'

Village elders

Village elders are experienced people whose perspective enables them to put current concerns into a larger context. They provide proof that the theories about behavior and values have a corresponding physical reality. Ideally they demonstrate the value of planning. When they don't, our confidence is shaken badly, and we lose faith in the tribal knowledge that we were taught.

The most interesting parts of life happen on the edges and at the transitions as one thing becomes another. We admire surfaces and contours. We revel in world-record accomplishments that expand the edges of what can be done in terms of speed, capacity, endurance. We immediately lose interest in the old record and concentrate on the boundary that the new record defines.

Oddly, we now find ourselves in a time when birth and death, the boundaries of our life experience, are resisted. We shun old people. We emphasize birth control and abortion to a degree never seen before in an effort to limit our contact with and responsibility for young people. We celebrate the center of our life span almost to the exclusion of its ends. In this way we lose much of the benefit our village elders can provide.

The role of village elders in a society reveals much about a society. We have largely forgotten to listen to old people, and they have largely forgotten how to teach.

Waste

The primary meaning of the word is "to destroy." Wasting money happens when we spend it without return of value.

Welfare

Welfare, according the dictionary, is "the condition of health, prosperity, and happiness." This definition bears little resemblance to welfare in the sense it is generally used to denote money given to those who are chronically dependent in an amount intended to keep them at or near a subsistence level.

Wholistic

An alternative spelling of holistic. Also see holism.

Win-win

Stephen Covey explains it well in *The 7 Habits of Highly Effective People*. The basic premise is that fruitful relationships are beneficial to all parties. Adversarial relationships in which there is a winner and one or more losers degrade the community to the ultimate detriment of everyone involved. These are win-lose relationships. Look at any society in which a handful of people control all the wealth. It results in a dirty, violent, unstable community in which the wealthy must live behind high walls. It also eliminates the use of imagination and creativity that would make the community a more interesting place for the wealthy to live.

One of the widespread misconceptions in the United States is that winning implies a loser. This is related to the pyramid metaphor. This is one possible metaphor, but it is not absolute or final. In general, business organizations are evolving away from this metaphor to one that can be diagrammed as a circle.

Lose-lose is worse still. This is a situation in which both sides destroy each other. Nobody wins.

Zero-sum

The mathematical construct of a situation in which a gain for one is necessarily a loss for someone else.

Appendix B —My great grandfather, Joseph Howell

Born February 17, 1857, died July 18, 1918
Served in Congress from March 4, 1903 through March 3, 1917

On the Art of Writing

The best authors have been known to spend a great deal of time, to the productions of a verse or an essay, in order to have their thoughts clothed in language that clearly and elegantly conveys the meaning intended. I mention this just to direct your attention to what care and revision is necessary for a beginner. When you sit down and try to write a description of anything with which you are familiar, or to narrate anything you have heard, no doubt you are perplexed and uncertain as to how to commence—but after you have written it once or twice, and corrected and revised it and then rewritten a few times, you are even then far from feeling satisfaction at your work, but you recognize at least improvement of the first effort. This course of painstaking careful thought and study and practice is absolutely necessary before a person can acquire ease and fluency whether in writing or speaking.

—Joseph Howell, Washington, D.C., March 2, 1904

A Eulogy

Published by the Salt Lake City *Herald Republican*,
July 20, 1918 on the death of Joseph Howell.

To those who knew him, Joseph Howell was more than a successful man in the political and business world; he was an embodiment of the best traditions and forces of his time and people. Modest to a fault, he was generously appreciative of the qualities of others. His experiences as a boy, struggling for an education and livelihood made his heart warm for the aspirations of youth. Many young men and women will recall the words of encouragement and the open purse of this generous benefactor.

He was broad-minded in his sympathies and found it not difficult to see the other man's point of view.

He was gentle in his judgment of others; he forgave before forgiveness was asked, and resentments and memories of wrongs faded fast from his mind.

He had a splendid supply of good humor and homely wisdom, which helped him through the perplexities of public and private affairs.

He knew intimately and had the confidence and respect of the men who shaped the course of public affairs in Congress during the last generation. The success that gives deep and lasting satisfaction was his in abundant measure. Domestic peace and joy, the greatest of human blessings, he possessed in lavish degree.

He leaves to perpetuate his splendid qualities a family that might well evoke the envy of a king.

Appendix C—Commentary on tax forms

There are more than 1,000 tax forms when you count the paperwork to deal with payroll taxes, excise taxes, and all the rest. The expense of printing, storing, and teaching people to read and process these forms is part of the wholistic view of the cost of operating this nation. It is a direct cost to employers, and an indirect cost to all taxpayers who pay the wages of government employees who do this work.

The form relating to passive losses was first used for tax year 1986 to accommodate that new twist in the tax code. This form is so complex that it baffled even engineers, who were trained in math, and who had done their own taxes for years. I know, because several of them became my clients. The Tax Reform Act of 1986 generated so many complex rules that the "highlights" fill 10 pages in a 671 page book titled *Explanation of Tax Reform Act of 1986*. Government complexity supports a layer of enterprise that operates between government and your tax professionals. This hidden layer is part of the cost of running government. It is a cost you pay when you pay your taxes.

In chapter five I referred to Schedule E in relationship to rental real estate. In addition to rental real estate, this form is also used to report income from royalties (oil, book, song, etc.), income and expenses from partnerships, estates, trusts, and S corporations. This is a comprehensive two-page form with more than a dozen pages of instruction. The visible portion of the paperwork—the part the taxpayer fills out—is just the tip of the proverbial iceberg. The hidden part is another expense of administering taxes. The complex instructions must be written, printed, and studied at length by the professionals helping you with your tax return. The government puts the taxpayer in the position to need a professional. Few, if any, nonprofessionals can cope with Schedule E.

Appendix D—The lighter side of Wholistic Taxes

Christopher Columbus

You might not know that Christopher Columbus was the world's first Democrat. Consider his trip to the New World:

- He left without knowing where he was going.
- He arrived without knowing where he was.
- He returned without knowing where he had been.
- He did it all on borrowed money.

Project for a rainy day

Get six thumbtacks and a matchbox. Put the tacks in the matchbox. You have just created a tacks shelter.

Will you take a check?

There is about $1,000,000,000,000 worth of currency in circulation, not enough to pay the $4,000,000,000,000 national debt. Will you take a check?

Hoot, Maughan!

Maughan is pronounced "mawn." I often hear maw-gun. People can pronounce Vaughan without any problem, but there is no Vaughan Maughan in the family. It is just as well, he might be called Vawgun Mawgun. Nor is there, to my regret, a Hoot Maughan or a Hey Maughan.

I have a granddaddy, David Izatt Stoddard, who was named after Alexander Spowart Izatt, his grandfather on his mother's side. I like that name Izatt. I can see my own grandson named after him: Izatt U. Maughan.

I have combed our family archives pretty thoroughly, but I find no evidence that my dear ancestor Morgan Morgan ever lived in Walla Walla, which is in Washington. He was born in 1813, and there may not have been a town by that name soon enough for him to live there.

Hooters, mon!

Chesty Love, known to her friends as Cynthia Hess, had gigantic implants put in her breasts to reach the impressive measurements of 57FF. She did it to add interest to her night club act. She and her accountant convinced a tax court judge that these were, in effect, costumes, not personal cosmetic surgery (which is not deductible and which cannot be depreciated). She was permitted to depreciate the implants. The accountant and the judge were women.

Acronyms

DINK: Dual income no kids

SINK: Single income nine kids

And he said...

❑   An accountant for the Magellan fund entered a $1,300,000,000 loss as a gain of the same amount. "People can make mistakes," said Fidelity Investments Managing Director J. Gary Burkhead in an article published in the *Los Angeles Times*.

All of my clients would recognize a billion dollar error right away.

If you think money can't buy happiness, you just don't know where to shop.

Notes

1. Hampden-Turner, Charles and Trompenaars, Alfonso, *The Seven Cultures of Capitalism, Value Systems for Creating Wealth in the United States, Japan, Germany, France, Britain, Sweden, and the Netherlands*, p 60.

2. Goldstein, Patrick, *Los Angeles Times*, July 31, 1994, Calendar, p 23.

3. Gatto, John Taylor, *Teacher Magazine*, August 1990, p 58.

4. Ragan, Tom, Drug Searches Proposed for Costa Mesa Schools, *Los Angeles Times*, August 31, 1994, p B4.

5. Their Fate is Sealed, *Press-Telegram* (Riverside, Calif.), August 24, 1994, p D1.

6. Paddock, Richard, A Long-Buried Oil Spill Casts Beach town Adrift, *Los Angeles Times*, September 28, 1994, p 1.

7. Zohar, Danah, *The Quantum Society*, p 222.

8. Henig, Robin Marantz, *A Dancing Matrix*, p 195.

9. Bennis, Warren, *Why Leaders Can't Lead*, p 20.

10. Congress: It's inefficient, but was designed that way, *Orange County Register*, August 28, 1994, p 30.

11. Osbon, Diane K., *A Joseph Campbell Companion*, p 58-59.

12. Pulliam, Liz, Questions, *Orange County Register*, December 2, 1994, News p 18.

13. Meyers, Laura, What's Your House Worth? *Los Angeles Magazine*, September 1994, pp 83-93.

14. See note 14.

15. *Orange County Business Journal*, June 13, 1994, p 11.

16. Spragins, Ellyn E., *Fixing a Piece of the Rock, The Pru: Has its CEO fumbled damage control?* August 8, 1994, p 36.

17. *Wine Business Insider*, August 27, 1994, 2.

18. Pullian, Liz, Compromise brings in TMI manager, *Orange County Register*, October 5, 1994, Business Section, p 1.

19. Barlett, Donald L. and Steele, James B., *America: Who Really Pays the Taxes?* p 257.

20. Johnson, Ervin "Magic", *My Life*, p 13.

21. Abdul-Jabbar, Kareem, *Giant Steps*, p 85.

22. Hardball is Still GM's Game, *Business Week*, August 8, 1994, p 26.

23. Banathan, Joyce, and Forney, Matt, Damping Labor's Fires, *Business Week*, August 1, 1994, pp 40-41.

24. Shapiro, Walter, *Time* magazine, August 22, 1994.

25. See note 1, page 32.

26. Axelrod, Robert, *The Evolution of Cooperation*, p 113.

27. See note 9, p 46.

28. Ryan, Nancy, Today's teens quite savvy about finances, survey reports, *Orange County Register*, December 30, 1991, p C5.

29. Bradshaw, John, *Creating Love*, p 219.

30. Aguayo, Rafael, *Dr. Deming, The American Who Taught the Japanese About Quality*, p 197.

31. Red Cross: Barbarity extensive in world, *Orange County Register*, May 19, 1994, p 22.

32. Wine Institute News Release, July 6, 1994

33. *Wine Business Insider*, Volume 4, Issue 27, July 30, 1994, p 2.

34. Limbaugh, Rush, *The Limbaugh Letter*, April 1994, p 3.

35. Russell, Cheryl, *100 Predictions for the Baby Boom*, p 44.

Attitude and philosophy

Care of the Soul, Thomas Moore, published by Harper Collins

Dan Wilson would take this book to the proverbial desert island of exile if he had to choose just one book. The references Moore makes to money and work are profoundly enlightening. The subtitle is "A guide for cultivating depth and sacredness in everyday life." It is an ambitious title, and delightfully, it is accurate. We have lost sight of the sacredness of wealth. It is our attempts to manipulate it rather than cherish it that causes much of our suffering.

Creating Affluence, Deepak Chopra, M.D., published by New World Library

This slender book consists largely of a series of meditations. Doctor Chopra says that using effort is unnecessary, and that simply being aware of the truth is sufficient to bring about the results we want. He is a bit of a tease because becoming aware of truth requires effort. But I quibble. This little volume is an excellent guide to upgrading our daily thoughts from worry to productivity and serenity. If you have any inclination to deny yourself permission to have it all, this book is an excellent antidote for your fears.

Revolution From Within, Gloria Steinem, published by Little, Brown

The sub-title is "A Book of Self-Esteem," and it is a fine one. Self-esteem is central to all money management issues. Women have been taught more misinformation than men, generally speaking, and much of it hammers at basic levels of self-respect. This book is good reading for women, and it is the best book I have found for helping men understand the pressures women face growing up in a male dominated society.

Techniques

Financial Planning for the Utterly Confused, Joel Lerner, published by McGraw-Hill, Inc.

Do you become annoyed at titles that ask you to proclaim your incompetence as eligibility for wanting the book? I do. If you can get past that objection, this book, written by a college professor, is handy for its simple presentation of many of the financial terms and concepts that appear in the daily newspaper, and which are important in your conversations with financial planners of all sorts. The book rates high in readability and its lack of hype.

Worth magazine

I recommend *Worth* for its readability, the range of topics it addresses, and for its well-intentioned and well-mannered skepticism of big business and government.

Therapy

Money Harmony, Resolving Money Conflicts in Your Life and Relationships, Olivia Mellan, published by Walker and Company.

Few psychologists counsel couples specifically in the area of money, which makes this book special. Mellan defines categories such as avoider and worrier. She also throws light on issues of money and gender.

When Money is the Drug, Donna Boundy, published by Harper Collins

Boundy examines addictions as they relate to money. The thorough reader might make a cursory study of addictions first, though this is not essential to understanding the text. A reading of John Bradshaw's *Healing the Shame that Binds You* is enlightening for those who do not have a working knowledge of how addictions operate. Boundy examines a wide range of troubled attitudes about money. She examines why some people actively resist saving money. She discusses people who describe themselves as "hemorrhaging money." There is lots of nitty-gritty material in the book, and it is good, if tough, reading for people with severe emotional issues connected to money.

Index

231